Currency and Interest Rate Swaps

Price and Henderson
Currency and
Interest Rate Swaps

Schuyler K. Henderson
John A. M. Price

London
Butterworths
1984

England	Butterworth & Co (Publishers) Ltd, 88 Kingsway, LONDON WC2B 6AB
Australia	Butterworths Pty Ltd, SYDNEY, MELBOURNE, BRISBANE, ADELAIDE, PERTH, CANBERRA and HOBART
Canada	Butterworth & Co (Canada) Ltd, TORONTO and VANCOUVER
New Zealand	Butterworths of New Zealand Ltd, WELLINGTON and AUCKLAND
Singapore	Butterworth & Co (Asia) Pte Ltd, SINGAPORE
South Africa	Butterworth Publishers (Pty) Ltd, DURBAN and PRETORIA
USA	Butterworth Legal Publishers, ST PAUL, Minnesota, SEATTLE, Washington, BOSTON, Massachusetts, AUSTIN, Texas and D & S Publishers, CLEARWATER, Florida

Printed in Great Britain
by Butler & Tanner Ltd, Frome and London

Foreword

International finance has undergone many changes in the past ten years in terms of both capital markets and bank credit markets, due to the rapid expansion in international trade and improvement in communications. Events such as the abolition of fixed exchange rates under the Bretton Woods agreement in the early 1970s, the oil price rise, double-digit inflation, deficit financing and unemployment, have led to volatile exchange rates and interest rates. No longer can one disregard the contingent risk associated with financing, for example, Dollar assets with Swiss Franc liabilities or fixed assets with floating liabilities.

Also new markets, such as those for futures and options for currencies, exchange rates, stocks, and commodities, have been established. Innovation in the capital markets has been prolific with the introduction and acceptance of interest warrants, zero-coupon bonds, extendable and retractable issues, drop-lock bonds and dual currency bonds to name but a few.

These markets and new products developed partly in response to the need to manage contingent risk, which due to currency and interest rate fluctuations, reached unacceptable levels. During the past ten years, a technique known as currency exchange or swap financing has also evolved to meet this need. Swap financing additionally provides the opportunity to exploit or arbitrage the anomalies and differences which exist between various markets, for example the Euro capital market versus the US capital market, or the Sterling capital market versus the foreign exchange market.

Whilst providing the answers to problems of hedging, and whilst having opened up many profitable opportunities for government borrowers, companies and investment banks alike, the growth of the swap markets has nonetheless placed additional burdens on all those involved. This arises because although the concepts behind swap transactions are inherently very simple, many of the actual transactions themselves have become quite complex. They demand an increasing knowledge of all the different markets involved by all the parties involved – even of markets which in simpler days appeared irrelevant to the organisations concerned. And the burden is added to, because greater opportunities to solve problems by using the new techniques also imply greater opportunity costs if you do not use them!

This book has been written from a practical, rather than theoretical, point of view. It considers the fundamental principles prior to analysing the actual products themselves, with the overall object of giving the reader a reasonably sophisticated understanding of swap financing techniques and their application. Detailed descriptions are given on how swaps can be structured; how costs are calculated; the accounting ramifications; and legal and documentation implications and requirements. The reader is encouraged towards applying the swap product as a problem-solving technique within his own business sphere.

The authors are both respected professionals in their own fields, and have had many years experience in the area of corporate and international finance.

I believe this book will prove invaluable to the student and professional alike, and will serve to provide the reader with an essential understanding of swap financing techniques and applications involving different financial products and markets.

Andrew Large

Preface

Many changes in the world's capital markets have taken place in the last ten years. One such change has been the investors' flight to quality, particularly with regard to investments of a fixed rate nature. As the requirement for capital by governments and government agencies has steadily increased, the small to medium sized companies and the lesser credits have been squeezed out of the fixed rate public capital markets and forced to rely more heavily on banks for their credit needs. Since traditionally it has been regarded as imprudent for companies to fund long-term assets with short term floating rate liabilities and since banks are reluctant to make fixed rate loans because their primary sources of funding are on a floating rate basis, small to medium sized companies have faced structural capital difficulties.

In addition, accounting bodies around the world have been grappling with the problems of foreign exchange exposure and its impact on corporate profits and balance sheets, an impact emphasised by freely floating foreign exchange rates. The management of foreign exchange exposure by multinational and international companies, given the wide fluctuations in both interest and exchange rates, has become a major problem. Quite often, accounting uncertainties have resulted in companies taking real measures to hedge what are only book losses.

The advent of interest and currency exchanges, which are more commonly known as 'swaps', was a response to these challenges. Swaps enable the lesser credit to simulate a fixed rate borrowing using its floating rate borrowing capability and they enable all corporations, financial institutions and governments to restructure their debt profile without refinancing. These instruments permit coverage of foreign exchange risk and access to a number of different capital markets, both of which may have previously been unavailable or available only at an unattractive cost. Problems of fluctuating exchange rates, imperfect capital markets, restrictive exchange control regulations and differing tax regulations and accounting standards can be solved through the application of swap techniques.

The swap is not just a product but a way of thinking involving general corporate finance principles. It allows for dimensional as opposed to lateral thinking, particularly where there is no apparent answer to a problem.

Some applications of the swap product are as follows:

* Arbitraging capital markets in order to reduce cost of funds either on a floating rate or fixed rate basis.
* Increasing the return on assets by transforming the nature of the underlying asset.
* Eliminating the risk associated with financing fixed rate or long-term assets with floating rate liabilities.
* Locking in windfall profits as a result of fluctuating exchange rates or interest rates.
* Hedging foreign net worth exposure on a long-term basis at a favourable time in the currency cycle.

* Profiting by exploiting an advantage in one market to make up for a weakness in another.
* Exploiting market anomalies in order to reduce cost of funds or increase return on assets.
* Maximising the subsidies available on export finance on a hedged basis.
* Contracting in strong currencies on a hedged basis in order to profit by the interest differential.
* Reducing the after tax cost of funds by shifting the interest rate burden from one tax jurisdiction to another.
* Restructuring assets and liabilities on a more tax efficient basis.
* Mobilising worldwide inter-company liquidity both in convertible and blocked currencies.
* Hedging long-term currency receipts and payments.

The object of this book is to give the reader an understanding and working knowledge of the swap product. It has been designed to show treasurers, chief financial officers and others involved in business and finance how to reduce an entity's cost of funds, increase its return on assets and reduce the interest rate risk associated with either funding fixed rate assets with floating rate liabilities or long-term assets with short-term liabilities. It also shows how profitably to arbitrage various anomalies which exist in the capital markets. With the trend to classify treasury departments as profit centres rather than service centres, the ability to manipulate assets and liabilities is gaining in significance.

This book traces the development of the swap market from the parallel loan, common in the late 1960s and early 1970s, to its latest innovation, the floating to floating debt swap. It also illustrates the interaction between the bank foreign exchange market, the bank loan market, the swap market and the securities or capital markets.

Understanding swaps requires a knowledge of discounted cash flows, or present value concepts, together with an appreciation of the different methods of calculating yields to maturity that prevail not only between the bank market and the securities market, but also between the world's different securities markets. A case study is considered for the main categories of swap (interest rate or coupon swaps, cross-currency fixed to fixed swaps, cross-currency fixed to floating swaps, same currency floating to floating swaps and cross-currency floating to floating swaps), highlighting the advantages for the parties involved and how each party's costs are determined. The risks of entering into a swap will be discussed, both from a legal and financial point of view, with an examination and measurement of potential exposure. In addition, terms and conditions, structures, legal documentation, accounting implications and the role of an intermediary bank are considered in detail.

Finally, the authors consider possible technical developments in, and applications of, the swap product in the future.

The authors would like to thank the following for their assistance: Jules Keller of Soditic SA, Peter Burrows of Ernest L. Davis and Co, Peter Wallman and Peter Howe of Peter Wallman & Co, Peter Young of Wallcorp Ltd, Max Neilson of Neilson Management Limited, Maurice Jacques of Continental Bank, Hans Von Meiss, formerly of Chase Manhattan Limited, Nigel Buchanan of Price Waterhouse & Co., Lemy Gresh and Jean-Louis Rihon of First Interstate Limited and Mr Price's Personal Secretary

Diane Mead; F. Martin Belmore and Mary C. Fontaine of the Chicago Office of Mayer, Brown & Platt; and Carol Haylett for her typing assistance in the London Office of Mayer, Brown & Platt.

In addition, portions of this book first appeared in: International Financial Law Review, in articles by Schuyler K. Henderson and by F. Martin Belmore; Euromoney, April 1983 in an article entitled 'The Delicate Art of Swaps' by John A.M. Price, Jules Keller and Max Neilson; and the Euromoney Special Financing Report on Swap Financing Techniques, in articles entitled 'The Development of the Market' by John Price and 'Cross-Currency Swap: Fixed-to-Floating Rate' by John Price and Jules Keller.

Finally, the authors have been personally involved in a number of transactions mentioned in the book. It should be emphasised that they have not used any confidential information obtained in the course of such participation and have used only such information as was publicly available through other sources.

November 1984   Schuyler K. Henderson
                                                                          John A.M. Price

JOHN A. M. PRICE

John A. M. Price former global head of swaps at Bankers Trust Company, has recently formed his own company, Exocal Securities Limited to provide consulting services particularly with regard to application of currency exchange financing (swap) techniques. Exocal is currently a consultant to First Interstate Limited, the Treasury Services arm of First Interstate Bank Corp, the seventh largest bank holding company in the U.S. Mr. Price is also managing director of Australsuisse Securities Limited, a joint venture company with Soditic SA, specialising in the generation of financial mandates in the field of international finance in Australia and New Zealand.

John Price was one of the pioneers of the swap product during his time at Continental Bank. At Bankers Trust, Mr. Price arranged the first cross-currency floating to fixed asset/debt swap and the first simultaneously syndicated Swiss Franc fixed rate loan and currency exchange agreement. Together with Mr. Henderson, he was responsible for introducing present value concepts for the determination of damages, now standard practice, into swap documentation.

Mr. Price commenced his merchant banking career with Glyn Mills. Prior to this, he was with Coopers & Lybrand both in Australia and the United Kingdom. Mr. Price is a fellow of the Institute of Chartered Accountants in Australia, and a Bachelor of Commerce from the University of Newcastle, New South Wales, Australia.

SCHUYLER K. HENDERSON

Schuyler K. Henderson is a partner of the Chicago based law firm of Mayer, Brown & Platt. He has been a resident partner in London since 1977, during which time he has worked closely with a number of major international financial institutions in developing the swap product.

Mr. Henderson received his law degree (J.D.) and M.B.A. from the University of Chicago in 1971. He is a member of the Illinois and New York bars.

Contents

CHAPTER 1

Evolution of the swap product and participants: overview

DEVELOPMENT

Early development

Perhaps the earliest form of swap financing took place long ago in the form of a local trader paying the local debts of a foreign trader, in return for that foreign trader paying the local trader's debts in the foreign trader's home country. Many modern traditional banking activities implicitly involve swap financing techniques, eg, a cash collateralised loan provided by a bank.

Central banks had been using what were essentially swap techniques for the support of one currency against another for some years, as had multinational companies, either by inter-company loans between subsidiaries incorporated in different countries or by parallel loans with subsidiaries of other multinationals.

The abolition in 1973 of the Bretton Woods Agreement on fixed exchange rates was the initial impetus for the development of more sophisticated swap financing techniques. The resulting wild fluctuation in exchange rates and interest rates, together with foreign exchange controls imposed by various governments, exposed commercial entities to greater uncertainties than those which had previously existed.

In the UK, the parallel loan (described in detail in chapter 2) became widely popular after the introduction of exchange controls, including the dollar premium, by the UK Government in order to protect foreign exchange reserves. The dollar premium discouraged foreign investment by UK entities by, in effect, imposing a tax on direct outward investment. For example, if a UK company wanted to invest £1,000,000 in the US equity market, it had to buy the dollars* necessary by selling pounds sterling for dollars in what was known as the dollar premium market. This meant that, if the premium was 20%, it would cost £1,200,000 to invest the equivalent of £1,000,000 in the US equity market. Upon selling the securities acquired, only 75% of the proceeds of sale could be sold through the dollar premium market for pounds sterling, the remaining 25% having to be sold through the spot market, ie, at the free market exchange rate prevailing on the day of sale for selling dollars for pounds sterling. Having initially to pay more for the US investments and then having to surrender 25% of the premium (effectively a tax) acted as a disincentive for foreign investment.

One way in which the premium could be avoided was to borrow abroad for investment. The parallel loan market thus developed, along with the

---

* References in this book to dollars are to US dollars unless otherwise stated.

banks' involvement as either arranger, intermediary (for cash collateralised loans) or guarantor. Merchant banks, investment banks and stockbrokers first became aware of the possibilities in this area in the 1970s, before the commercial banks recognised the significance of the product and related fee income because of falling profit margins on traditional loan business. Stockbrokers and merchant banks such as Phillips & Drew, Cazenove, Kleinwort Benson and Hill Samuel started arranging parallel loans particularly for the investment trusts. Under these arrangements, the UK investment trust would lend pounds to the UK subsidiary of a US company, in return for the US company lending dollars to the UK investment trust. Arrangement fees at that time ranged anywhere from $\frac{1}{2}\%$ to 1% per party, which was lucrative business for the arrangers. Commercial banks at that time were aware of the product but few recognised the possibility for earning substantial fee income.

In the back-to-back loan (see below), two agreements were generally required and, even if contained in one document, two distinct sets of rights and obligations arose. The parallel loan presented additional difficulties since the borrowers and lenders were separate entities. Documentation proliferated since, to assure each party its maximum protection, each parent would guarantee the loan made to its subsidiary by the other parent and pledge its rights to receive money from its borrower as security for that guarantee. Even if the loans were between the same entities and structured under one agreement (in which case they are referred to as back-to-back loans), the resulting concern about set-off rights and blockage of funds on one side raised the spectre of one party being required to repay its loan while the other party was prevented (either by exchange controls or insolvency laws) from repaying the other loan. This of necessity generally involved close attention to the secured transaction and insolvency laws of several jurisdictions and burdensome documentation. Although front-end fees in terms of arranging parallel loans took on new significance for banks and merchant banks, the security aspects associated with these loans hindered the development of the product and the involvement of the professionals.

Evolution to swaps

The swap evolved as a means of simplifying the back-to-back loan, improving the security situation and taking the transaction off the balance sheet. Although cash flows in a currency swap may be the same as in a back-to-back loan (see Chapter 2), a currency swap, as a contractual obligation entered into by two parties to sell one currency forward against delivery of another currency at a future date, in essence was a medium to long-term forward foreign exchange contract. Since payments are structured as conditional matching payments, the parties generally felt that they received greater security.

Apart from the security and accounting aspect of swaps, swaps evolved in response to particular problems and to opportunities presented by arbitrage.

First, extreme volatility of interest rates and exchange rates throughout the world, coupled with the increasing volume of international trade and investment and the almost instant worldwide communication of economic and business news, presented finance ministers and chief financial officers with large financing and exposure problems. In a market economy, the existence of such problems results in people attempting to find ways to solve them.

Second, with instant communication between the world's various capital markets, trading taking place on a 24 hour basis and the insatiable financial requirements of governments, government agencies, supranationals and multinationals, the demand for money at the lowest price, regardless of which capital market, has become preeminent. Consequently, if an entity could exploit an anomaly or arbitrage between capital markets in order to reduce its cost of funds, it would do so.

EARLY SWAPS

According to market sources, the first genuine swap was arranged in August 1976 between Bos Kalis Westminster Group NV and ICI Finance Limited. Continental Illinois Limited advised Bos Kalis, and Goldman Sachs advised ICI. No publicity was given to this transaction in order to protect the proprietary nature of the product. It was interesting to note that the introduction of the product came after the first substantial shake-up in the capital markets in 1974/75. The advent of double-digit interest rates and volatile exchange rates took its toll with many UK merchant banks (some of which were established by US and other foreign banks) ending up in serious financial trouble. But for the intervention of the Bank of England, through a support system which became known as the 'life-boat', the secondary banking system may have collapsed. In order to generate income and maintain growth, emphasis changed from the pursuit of income-producing new assets to the non-asset utilisation fee income.

Not until Continental Illinois Limited, now First Interstate Limited, published a 'tombstone' for a US dollar/sterling 10 year currency swap for $25,000,000 on behalf of Consolidated Goldfields Limited in April 1977 did the banking community sit up and take note. Not long after that, particulars began to filter out about the jumbo swap arranged for the Venezuelan Government. Under this swap, the Venezuelan Government (which had accumulated dollars from the sale of oil) sold dollars forward for French francs in order to meet its French franc contract commitments for the construction of the Caracas rail system. It is understood that this swap was arranged by Morgan Guaranty and Banque Paribas.

The major problem for the development of the swap product was one of acceptance. Companies, governments, banks and other financial institutions mistrusted this new product. The tax position was unclear and existing accounting principles did not provide for treatment of swaps. One large merchant bank was known for telling its clients it was not involved with swaps and only specialised in parallel loans.

In the early development of the swap product, the major players among the banks were Continental Illinois, Citibank, Morgan Guaranty and Banque Paribas, while the most active merchant and investment banks included Goldman Sachs, Morgan Stanley and Hill Samuel.

Citibank, Morgan Guaranty and Banque Paribas turned swap financing into a major product area, and banks such as Bankers Trust and Manufacturers Hanover formed new departments. More investment banks became involved, particularly Salomon Brothers, Credit Suisse First Boston and Merrill Lynch. The continuing drive for the generation of fee income, together with the publicity, attracted more and more entrants into the market.

The first major publicity breakthrough came with the publication of particulars about the IBM/World Bank swap in 1981, under which World Bank agreed to service IBM's outstanding Swiss franc and Deutschemark debt in return for IBM servicing World Bank's dollar debt. This transaction, which was arranged by Salomon Brothers, allowed IBM to lock-in a large capital profit on its foreign borrowings due to the appreciation of the dollar. In retrospect, with the exchange rate currently standing at $1 = DM3.07, IBM did not maximise its profit potential. By entering into the swap it locked in a known profit, gave up the opportunity of further profits and eliminated the risk of future losses.

Theoretically, the interest rate swap should have preceded the currency swap. In fact, the interest swap developed out of the currency swap, and occurred in the context of a currency swap in June 1981. Bankers Trust arranged and acted as an intermediary in a fixed rate yen/floating rate dollar swap with Renault Holding SA and Renault Acceptance BV on the one side and a Japanese entity on the other side.

Continental Illinois and Citibank are reported subsequently to have arranged unpublicised swaps involving exchange of floating and fixed rate dollars. The major publicity breakthrough for interest swaps, however, came with the publication in 1982 of details of the Deutsche Bank Luxembourg interest rate swap which was arranged through Merrill Lynch and Credit Suisse First Boston. Interest swaps had the effect of simplifying the swap concept and illustrating one of its exceptional applications, ie, the arbitraging of the capital market against the bank credit market. Banks and investment banks gradually found themselves at a competitive disadvantage if they were unable to provide financial services and advice in this area. More importantly, the major Eurobond houses found that, in order to maintain their market share or lead position, they had to be involved in the swap product. Today, probably one in three fixed-rate Eurobond issues are swap related.

The technical superiority of the swap over the parallel loan, because of the security aspects, combined with the publicity given to them, the quality of the parties, the increasing volume of business, and the clarification of tax and accounting aspects, all contributed to the international acceptance and current popularity of the product. The commercial banks, merchant banks and investment banks, in their endeavour to generate fee income, have used their inventiveness to develop additional applications which they in turn have sold to their clients. Rather like the multiplier effect, the more applications that are possible, the more deals are created and the greater the acceptability and so on.

RECENT INNOVATIONS

Today, swaps can be roughly grouped into five main categories:

  (i) interest rate or coupon swaps, ie, same currency floating to fixed swaps;
 (ii) cross-currency fixed-to-fixed swaps;
(iii) cross-currency fixed-to-floating swaps;
 (iv) same currency floating-to-floating swaps;
  (v) cross-currency floating-to-floating swaps.

New applications of swaps are continually being developed. Recent examples are:

— the ability to write lease contracts on a hedged basis in countries where tax regulations in the form of capital allowances, accelerated depreciation, and the like are favourable;
— the arbitraging of capital markets by borrowing in one currency in order to generate another currency by attaching a hedge or swap to a bond issue, thereby permitting corporations to generate a desired currency at a cheaper all-in cost than borrowing the currency directly;
— the ability to take advantage of subsidised government financing from, for example, export credit agencies, while eliminating currency exposure through a swap; and
— the opportunity to generate foreign assets by buying domestic securities and coupling the purchase with a swap contract.

Another innovation has been the unwinding of swaps. For a number of UK companies, the abolition of exchange controls by the UK government eliminated the sole reason for their entering into a swap. A number of these companies have unwound swaps.

THE PARTICIPANTS

There were a number of important milestones which serve as highlights in considering the evolution of the various financial classifications of end-users of the swap product.

Corporations

Three major factors contributed to the popularity of swaps in the corporate sector. First, as discussed above, was the introduction of the dollar premium in the UK. It was believed that if the dollar premium were abolished, it would be the end of swaps. As it happened, in addition to avoiding the dollar premium, swaps provided a hedge against investing in foreign assets. Upon the dollar premium being zero rated (which means that for the moment it no longer is applicable), swaps continued to gain in popularity mainly because of this hedging aspect.

The second factor which boosted the swap was the introduction in the US of the Financial Accounting Standards Board's Statement of Financial Accounting Standards Number 8 (Stamford, Conn., FASB 1975), known as FASB/8. Under this standard, US companies were forced to write off translation gains and losses through the profit and loss account, thereby affecting earnings per share. Given the gyrations in exchange rates in recent years, FASB/8 dramatically affected the earnings record of many multi-nationals. The swap proved to be an efficient way of solving the problem of foreign exchange or translation exposure.

One of the criticisms of FASB/8 was that it forced companies to take real actions to hedge book losses. Ultimately, FASB/8 was abolished in favour of FASB/52. Under FASB/52, only certain realised foreign exchange gains and losses flow through profit and loss accounts, while foreign net worth translation exposure is now accounted for by an adjustment to reserves, which only affects the balance sheet.

This regulatory change in itself provided another opportunity to apply the swap product. For example, a US company with a positive net worth exposure in a low interest rate country, eg, Switzerland, could through the swap transform high interest rate liabilities (eg, French francs) into low interest rate Swiss franc liabilities, with the corresponding interest rate saving reflected through the profit and loss account, thereby boosting earnings per share.

The third factor was the gradual squeezing out of the corporate borrower from the fixed rate capital markets by governments and government agencies through their increasing borrowing requirements. Weaker corporate credits' ability to generate fixed-rate liabilities suffered, but the interest rate swap emerged as an alternative. Weaker corporate credits provided logical counterparties for banks for interest rate swaps (see below).

Financial institutions

To date, the main users of the swap product have been the commercial banks, for their own account, and the finance companies. Insurance companies have used the product to a lesser extent, and are expected to use them more in the future. For example, CIGNA recently used the swap as a funding and hedging technique in connection with the acquisition of a company in the UK. Again, pension funds have only used the product to a limited extent, but are expected to use the product increasingly in the future.

The most active participants in the swap market for their own account are the non-dollar banks. The prime reason for this is that many central banks force the various banks under their jurisdiction to borrow medium-term dollar liabilities for funding term floating rate assets, as opposed to their current practice of financing these assets with a six-month Eurodollar deposit. Through the swap mechanism, the banks have been able to use their fixed-rate term dollar borrowing ability to transform the resulting fixed-rate liabilities into simulated term floating-rate liabilities at an attractive margin under the rate at which deposits are offered in the London interbank market ('LIBOR').

The next major step in the development of this product will be use by the banks themselves as they gradually work towards centralising their treasury operations, using the swap product as a treasury tool for managing their assets and liabilities and reducing interest exposure. Banks such as Morgan Guaranty, Chase Manhattan Bank, Bankers Trust and First Interstate Bancorp are well advanced in this area. Today, most of the large international banks, merchant banks and investment banks either have their own departments involved on the arrangement side or use the product for their own accounts.

In addition, the commercial banks have become increasingly active in the swap market as intermediaries. A bank intermediary can offer the following services in arranging swap financings:

— advice on the appropriate structure;
— recommendations as to pricing;
— assistance with negotiations between parties;
— arrangement of the necessary legal documentation;
— handling the disbursements on behalf of both parties;
— reference bank for rate settings;
— setting up of escrow paying arrangements, if required;
— obtaining any necessary regulatory approvals;
— assistance in preparation of board and other interval presentations.

The bank intermediary can also act as:

— agent – introduce complementary partners and arrange transactions directly between these partners;
— intermediary – stand between two counterparties, thereby eliminating the commercial risk inherent in contracts written directly between two parties and providing anonymity for the counterparties involved;
— principal – arrange swap financing directly with a counterparty for the bank's own account.

Supranationals

World Bank has done more than any other party to promote the swap product since its acceptance of this mechanism as a financing technique in 1981. Its dollar/Swiss franc/Deutschemark debt swap with IBM will no doubt become a textbook case study. This type of swap is considered in greater detail in Chapter 4 under 'cross-currency fixed-to-fixed swaps'.

World Bank has found certain applications of the swap product to be an excellent problem solver. It has a declared policy of raising funds in currencies with low interest rates, eg, Swiss francs, yen, Deutschemarks and Dutch guilders. This has created problems since its appetite for borrowing in those currencies over a long and continuing period of time is greater than the respective capital markets can support. For example, World Bank has issued so much Swiss franc fixed-rate debt that every portfolio in Switzerland holds or is long of World Bank paper. Consequently World Bank must pay premium rates in that market, compared with other AAA borrowers.

The swap has proved an ideal solution for World Bank, as the only capital markets in the world large enough to support World Bank's demand for funds are the dollar denominated Eurobond market and the US domestic market. World Bank has taken advantage of the anomaly that Swiss franc debt issued by US companies is much sought after by Swiss investors. Certain borrowers, such as Philip Morris, a credit not as highly rated by the credit agencies as World Bank, can borrow Swiss francs as cheaply, if not more cheaply, than World Bank. In the dollar market, however, this is not the case.

Under these circumstances, an ideal opportunity exists for World Bank, probably through a bank intermediary, to act as a surrogate borrower of fixed-rate dollars for, say Philip Morris, and for Philip Morris to act as a surrogate borrower of fixed-rate Swiss francs for World Bank. Through the swap mechanism, Philip Morris would end up with a simulated fixed rate dollar debt at an all-in cost less than if it were to borrow dollars directly, and similarly World Bank would end up with a simulated Swiss franc liability at a lesser all-in cost.

All the major banks, including the merchant and investment banks, are now constantly scouring the earth to find other Philip Morrises in order to do business with World Bank. World Bank's pedigree, publicity and bank marketing aggression have played a major part in acceptance by the supranationals of the swap product. Recently World Bank has decided it can use its floating rate dollar borrowing ability, which widens the number of applications of the swap and increases World Bank's fund raising alternatives.

Export credit agencies

Apart from Swedish Export Credit, most of the world's export credit agencies have been slow to recognise the potential of the swap product for reducing their cost of funds, or enabling them to lend to exporters in currencies other than that of their home jurisdictions. To date, it has mainly been the corporate borrower which has benefited by accepting subsidised export credit from the various agencies and then swapping out of a fixed-rate debt in one currency into a fixed-rate liability in another currency.

Certain agencies are also prepared to lend at a subsidised rate in more than one currency. Under these circumstances, companies should always borrow in the currency carrying the biggest interest rate subsidy. This would generate a cheap liability which, through the swap mechanism, could be sold for a profit which could be used to subsidise a borrowing in another desired currency.

A major function of the export credit agencies should be their willingness to lend in currencies other than their home currency. However, they may not always be in a position to raise fixed rate money in the desired currency. The swap, as Swedish Export Credit has shown, can permit an agency to borrow in one capital market and convert its liabilities into a currency in which no fixed-rate capital market exists or is closed because of market conditions.

Governments and government agencies

Among the last types of institutions to use the swap product for its own account are governments and government agencies. Apart from Austria and central bank operations of various other countries, few governments have considered the swap technique as an efficient method of funding government deficits. Many opportunities exist, as many governments are not of a sufficiently high credit rating to enable them to borrow in the fixed rate capital markets. Such governments, however, do have the ability to borrow on a floating-rate basis and could prove suitable counterparties for banks in interest rate swaps. This would allow governments to use their floating-rate borrowing power to simulate fixed rate liabilities.

Again, because of their borrowing requirements, governments are not only interested in one form of floating-rate finance but need to tap different capital markets. This need has given rise to floating-to-floating interest rate swaps which can provide an opportunity for governments better to manage their debt positions. According to market sources, Denmark and Ireland are two governments which have used the swap for borrowing purposes. It is expected that the number of governments using this technique will grow substantially in the future.

Conclusion

Today, the swap product has gained credibility because of the number of quality entities which have now used it as a financial tool. Government bodies such as Swedish Export Credit and Sallie Mae, supranationals such as World Bank, multinationals such as IBM and financial institutions such as Deutsche Bank, Bank of Tokyo and Austrian Kontrollbank have all used the product either to borrow more efficiently or to arbitrage capital markets.

CHAPTER 2

The technical evolution of swaps

PARALLEL LOANS AND SWAPS

As mentioned above, swaps grew out of the parallel and back-to-back loan. The difference between the two is one of structure. Under a parallel loan, A (US) would lend dollars to b (US) in return for B (France), parent of b (US), lending French francs to a (France), subsidiary of A (US). Under a back-to-back structure, A (US) would lend dollars to B (France) in return for B (France) lending French francs to A (US).

Parallel loans and back-to-back loans can be diagramatically represented as follows:

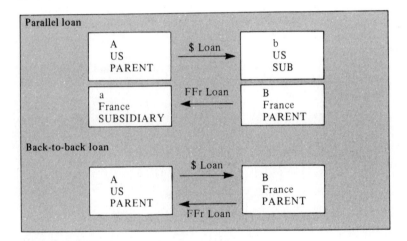

A US   = US Parent
b US   = US Subsidiary of French Parent
a France = French Subsidiary of US Parent
B France = French Parent

If we consider a five year back-to-back loan from a cash flow point of view, the following is the initial cash movement:

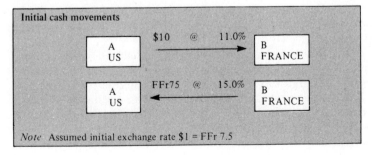

At the outset, A lends $10 to B and B lends FFr 75 to A, both loans having terms of five years. Assume that the respective loans were priced in line with yields on government bonds, that is:

5 Years	*%*
France	15.00
US	11.00

In five years, cash flows will reverse, in that B will repay its $10 to A and A will repay its FFr 75 to B, as follows:

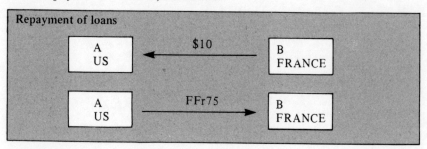

Considering the repayment of the principal of the respective loans by itself, we could regard this as a forward sale of French francs by A for dollars on the one hand and a forward sale of dollars by B for French francs on the other.

The cash flows for a 'cash swap' (one involving an initial exchange of monies at a then spot rate and a re-exchange of these monies at the agreed rate) can be set out as follows:

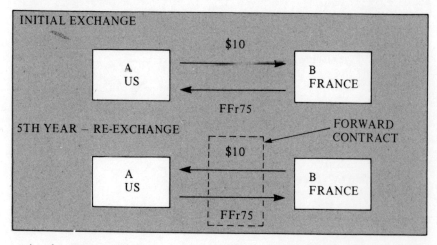

An important conclusion emerges: back-to-back loans and currency swaps, although structured and documented differently, involve the same principal cash flows.

At this point it is worthwhile considering the major difference between the swap and a back-to-back loan. Back-to-back loans involve two separate loan agreements. For rights of set-off to be enforceable to the fullest possible degree (which even then does not allow complete assurance of immediate enforcement in all cases), it is necessary to comply with the secured transactions laws of the relevant jurisdiction. This may cause problems, inter alia, with negative pledge clauses of other documents. If rights of set-off are not so perfected, a solvent party could be forced to pay back the loan from the bankrupt party while only ranking as an unsecured creditor with regard to its loan to the bankrupt party.

One of the major reasons for the evolution of the swap was that swaps overcome this problem, as a swap agreement depends on future perform- ance. For instance, in the cash swap example, A agrees to sell forward FFr 75 to B in return for B selling forward $10 to A. The documentation ① is written in such a manner that B's obligation to deliver is conditional on A's delivery. If A fails to deliver FFr 75 to B, B is not obligated to deliver $10 to A. In this event, B would only incur a loss if it could not sell $10 for FFr 75 at that time. B would, of course, have rights under the agreement to sue for any shortfall.

The other major difference between swaps and back-to-back loans, and a major reason for evolution of the swap, is an accounting point. Back- to-back loans are 'on balance sheet' whereas swaps are forward contingent ② commitments and consequently 'off balance sheet'. Depending on whether they are considered material or not, swaps may need to be reported by way of a note to the accounts.

A further major structural difference between a swap and a back-to-back loan is that, in a currency swap, no initial cash movements are necessary, since the swap is normally based on spot rates at the date of effectiveness. Thus, the parties could obtain any currencies in the regular spot market. This will be considered in depth later when considering the reasons for this development of the swap product.

FOREIGN EXCHANGE MARKETS AND SWAPS

A currency swap can substitute for a foreign exchange contract in providing a hedge/cover against revaluation losses on foreign assets, liabilities or future income streams and cash payment arising from fluctuating currency exchange rates.

When a company hedges its foreign currency exposure with a swap, it foregoes the possibility of making profits on such exposure but at the same time it also eliminates the risk of making a loss.

For example, if a UK company were to buy a DM 1000 one year bond at par for a sterling cost of £250 (prevailing exchange rate £1 = DM 4), at the end of the company's financial year it would be obliged to revalue this asset at the then prevailing Deutschemark/pound exchange rate. If by year-end the Deutschemark had devalued against the pound from DM 4 to DM 4.25, the company would incur a revaluation loss on the DM bond of £14.71 calculated as follows:

	DM	*Exchange* Rate £1 =	£
Initial cost of acquiring bond	1000	DM 4.00	250.00
Value of bond at year-end	1000	DM 4.25	235.29
Translation/revaluation loss			£14.71

If, at the time of purchasing the bond, the UK company had entered into a Deutschemark/pound currency swap under which it agreed to sell DM 1000 forward to a third party in return for the third party selling £250 to the UK company, the UK company would have hedged the above DM exposure. The hedge arises as the UK company would have a revaluation profit on the currency swap calculated as follows:

	DM	*Exchange Rate £1 =*	£
(1) Swap contract			
Sale of DM	1000	N/A	
Purchase of sterling			250.00
As compared with:			
(2) Cost of acquiring DM through foreign exchange market			
Sale of DM for sterling	1000	DM 4.250	235.29
Profit on swap contract			£14.71

The swap contract in essence is a modified form of a forward foreign exchange contract. In the event of exchange rate movements after the date of entering into the swap contract, the contract will have a positive value if the currency it is selling forward devalues and a negative value if the currency revalues. The inherent positive or negative value of such contracts will offset translation/revaluation profits/losses on foreign currency assets and liabilities. The above example illustrates this from the point of view of asset exposure. Here a translation/revaluation loss of £14.71 on the DM bond is offset by a profit of £14.71 on the swap contract.

Swaps and forward foreign exchange contracts are thus virtually identical in that they are both contracts to buy and sell currencies at some future date, except that foreign exchange contracts have traditionally run for up to three to five years only. Cross-currency swaps tend to take over where there is no long-term forward foreign exchange market.

Swaps, because they are usually medium to long term (five to ten years) and for substantial amounts, usually involve more detailed documentation (see Chapter 7) than foreign exchange contracts, which involve little documentation. Apart from the language covering the actual contractual liability to buy and sell currencies in the future, other swap clauses tend to resemble those contained in standard bank loan agreements but in a reduced form. Other special clauses include provisions for escrow paying instructions, which can eliminate the delivery risk normally associated with foreign exchange contracts, and liquidated damages in event of default. The latter involves present value concepts.

EVOLUTION OF PRICING OF SWAPS

So far we have compared swaps with parallel loans and foreign exchange contracts and highlighted certain documentation differences. We have not, however, addressed the question of cost or pricing. The cost of a parallel loan, foreign exchange contract or swap are all a function of interest rates.

In an earlier example we examined the cash flows for the repayment of principal under a back-to-back loan and concluded that swaps and back-to-back loans, although structured differently, involve the same cash flows. The following schedule sets out the cash flows under the back-to-back loan example already cited, but including interest payments.

Period	Amount Paid By B France to A US US$ (11%)	Amount Paid By A US to B France FFr (15%)
Initial Payment		
0	+10	+75
Future Payments		
1	−1.10	−11.25
2	−1.10	−11.25
3	−1.10	−11.25
4	−1.10	−11.25
5	−1.10	−11.25
5	−10.00	−75.00

The same logic applies in pricing a swap as for a back-to-back loan. The pricing mechanism for a swap has to account for the interest differential, ie, the fact that interest on the French franc loan is 15% and on the dollar loan is 11%.

In the above cash swap example, one would expect an annual interest differential of 4% to be paid by A to B. In effect this compensates B for parting with a potentially higher earning/yielding currency (government bond yields in France being higher than in the US).

The above logic also applies to the foreign exchange market in that premiums or discounts on the forward sale of one currency for another are determined by interest differentials. For instance, if one could borrow dollars at 11%, sell them spot and invest the proceeds in a French franc asset yielding 15%, provided one can sell French francs forward at the initial spot exchange rate, it would be possible to earn an additional 4% at no risk. Forward premiums and discounts do get out of line from time to time and banks take advantage of these situations for funding purposes. Consequently, in a free market, these anomalies are quickly arbitraged away.

Of course, long-term market practices and short-term market practices are not entirely compatible. Generally speaking, bond yields are used as benchmarks in determining the pricing of swaps. At times, however, other factors such as supply and demand, government policy and regulations and creditworthiness also play a part in determining the price. The principles involved in the pricing of swaps will become more apparent in the case studies used to examine the various forms of swap.

The earliest swaps accounted for the interest differential through use of an annual fee, paid by the party selling forward the currency with the higher interest rate. In the above example, Party A would have paid an annual fee of 4% to Party B. The Bank of England, however, soon required an alternate formula which in effect required payment of the two interest rates at a gross rate and then netted them out at spot exchange rates current at the time of payment. The effect of the formula is to lock in a local currency fixed rate financing cost for the currencies involved. Set out below is the formula which the Bank of England insisted on being used for the calculation of annual fees in relation to currency swap transactions involving sterling, prior to the abolition of exchange controls.

Annual fee

$$= \text{\$ Amount} \times \text{\$ Interest \%} \text{ less } \frac{\text{DM Amount} \times \text{DM Interest \%}}{\text{Future \$/DM Exchange Rate}}$$

Where:

Future exchange rate = $/DM exchange rate prevailing two days prior to fee payment date.

The following example illustrates the working of the formula and proves that it locks-in local currency fixed rate financing costs.

Party A enters into a cross currency fixed-to-fixed three-year debt swap with Party B under which Party A agrees to sell DM250 to Party B in return for Party B selling $100 to Party A. Both parties agree to the payment of an annual fee to be calculated in accordance with the Bank of England formula. Particulars of the swap are as follows:

Example

DM amount	= DM 250	Future Exchange Rate:
$ amount	= $100	Year 1 $1 = DM 2.50
DM interest rate	= 10.5%	Year 2 $1 = DM 1.25
$ interest rate	= 15%	Year 3 $1 = DM 3.75

$$\boxed{A} \quad \overset{\text{DM P}+\text{I}}{\underset{\text{\$P}+\text{I}}{\rightleftarrows}} \quad \boxed{B}$$

Calculation of fee

Year 1

$$\$100 \times 15\% - \frac{\text{DM}250 \times 10\tfrac{1}{2}\%}{\text{DM}2.5} = \text{Fee}$$

$15 $-\$10\tfrac{1}{2}$ = $4.50

Therefore $4.50 is payable by B to A

Year 2

$15 $-\$21$ $= -\$6.00$

Therefore $6.00 is payable by A to B

Year 3

$15 $-\$7$ = $8.00

Therefore $8.00 is payable by B to A

Total amount in dollar terms payable by B

(ie, Deutschemark interest in dollar terms plus fee)

(a) Deutschemark interest on bond at $10\tfrac{1}{2}\%$ DM	(b) Future exchange	(a)÷(b)=(c) Dollar equivalent $	(d) Fee (see above) $	(c)+(d)=(e) Total dollar payment $
26.25	2.50	10.50	4.50	15.00
26.25	1.25	21.00	−6.00	15.00
26.25	3.75	7.00	8.00	15.00

As can be seen from the above calculations, the interest cost of servicing the simulated dollar loan, in dollar terms, is always $15.00 (or 15%). Abolition of UK foreign exchange controls meant the Bank of England formula was no longer required. It is still used from time to time in order to simulate true borrowing cost. The same result is more customarily reached today by the parties agreeing to exchange defined amounts (determined implicitly by interest rates) on the annual or semi-annual payment dates.

ELIMINATION OF ACTUAL SETTLEMENTS

Swaps have developed from cash swaps, which required an initial exchange of currencies, to swaps which do not require any exchange of currencies. Following is an example using a Belgian company ('B Co') which enters into a currency swap with a US company ('US Co') under which B Co sells forward dollars to US Co in return for Belgian francs.

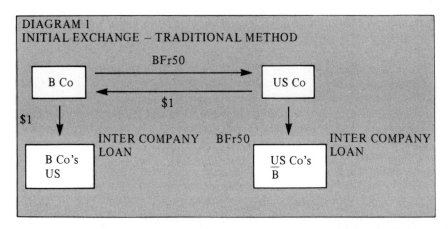

DIAGRAM 1
INITIAL EXCHANGE – TRADITIONAL METHOD

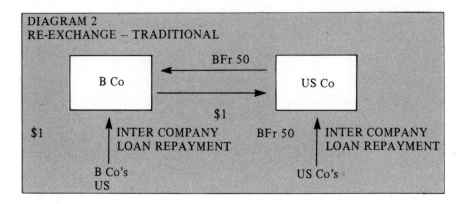

DIAGRAM 2
RE-EXCHANGE – TRADITIONAL

Diagrams 1 and 2, above, represent the traditional structure of a currency exchange. In the example we have assumed that B Co and US Co enter into a currency exchange agreement for five years whereby B Co will initially exchange BFr 50 with US Co in return for US Co exchanging dollars 1 with Belgian francs. Normally the dollars and Belgian francs would be on-lent to the respective subsidiaries unless the proceeds were to be used directly by the parent. Diagram 1 assumes inter-company loans.

Diagram 2 represents the re-exchange in five years with B Co and US Co having agreed to re-exchange currencies in the initial amounts regardless of the future exchange rate, ie, B Co gives US Co $1 in exchange for US Co giving B Co BFr 50.

The most important part of a currency exchange agreement is the re-exchange in five years between B Co and US Co. Diagram 3, on page 16, shows this re-exchange without the inter-company loans which are separate transactions from the currency exchange agreement. The importance of this re-exchange is that exposure arises in B Co's case, for example, when it acquires dollar assets with the dollars received. If the asset acquired, when

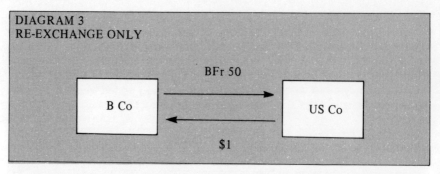

DIAGRAM 3
RE-EXCHANGE ONLY

translated, is worth less than BFr 50 then B Co would incur a translation loss. However, the above re-exchange means that no matter what the exchange rate is in the future, US Co will give B Co BFr 50 in return for $1. Consequently, any loss arising on the translation of the dollar asset will be off-set by B Co's revaluation of the currency exchange agreement. The hedging effect of swaps is dealt with in greater detail below.

Let us assume that US Co does not really want BFr 50; it only wants the re-exchange portion set out in Diagram 5, below. If B Co does require dollars, it can achieve this through a spot sale of Belgian francs for dollars

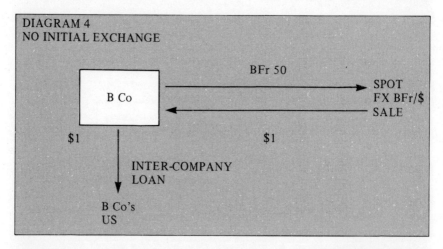

DIAGRAM 4
NO INITIAL EXCHANGE

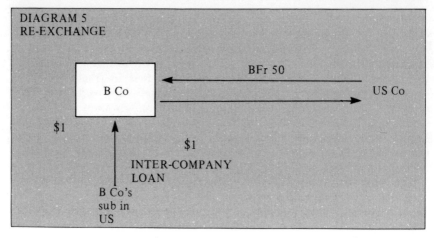

DIAGRAM 5
RE-EXCHANGE

through the foreign exchange market as represented in Diagram 4, on page 16. In this diagram we have assumed B Co would lend the dollar proceeds to its US subsidiary after the spot transaction by way of a dollar inter-company loan. Again, B Co would have exposure when translating the dollar assets acquired but, as previously explained, the currency exchange agreement (Diagram 5) can be revalued to off-set any translation exposure.

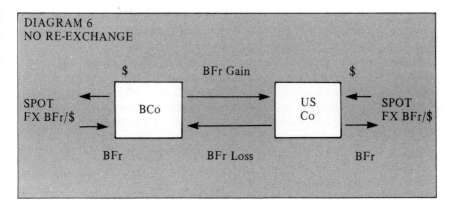

DIAGRAM 6
NO RE-EXCHANGE

We have now covered the situation where no initial exchange of curren-cies takes place. In addition, a swap can be structured so that no re-exchange need take place (see Diagram 6, above). Under these circum-stances, 'alternate performance' will be required in the agreement.

First, assuming that in five years B Co could sell $1 for BFr 50 the two parties would not need an agreement to re-exchange. B Co could keep the $1 and US Co the BFr 50 as B Co could sell that $1 for BFr 50, the initial amount it sold to generate $1. Conversely, US Co could sell BFr 50 for $1. In this case both companies are in exactly the same position as they were on the date of entering into the agreement five years earlier and neither would incur a profit or loss if they agreed to keep one another's currencies.

Next, assuming that B Co and US Co decide to sell one another's cur-rencies and that B Co could only sell $1 for BFr 40, B Co has a loss of BFr 10. If US Co agreed to pay B Co these BFr 10, then B Co would, in effect, get back BFr 50, which is what the agreement requires. In this case, if US Co keeps the BFr 50, it obviously can sell them for more than $1. The effect of US Co paying B Co an additional BFr 10 is that it is paying the profit back to B Co. This is correct as, through a currency exchange agree-ment, both parties in effect agree not to speculate in currency movements. They have eliminated the risk of either making a loss or a chance to make a profit on the currencies involved.

Finally, if B Co could sell $1 for BFr 60 and B Co were to pay BFr 10 to US Co, US Co would be in a non profit/loss situation. It would be left holding BFr 50 and if B Co gave it an additional BFr 10, the sum could be sold for $1, the amount US Co was due to receive under the currency exchange agreement.

Therefore, provided in the fifth year one party pays the 'BFr difference' to the other party (depending on whether the dollar has appreciated or depreciated against the Belgian franc), the result would be exactly the same as if B Co had given US Co $1 in return for US Co giving B Co BFr 50. The payment of only the difference is referred to as 'alternate performance' or 'netting'.

We have now moved from an initial exchange and re-exchange of currencies to (2) no initial exchange, but only a re-exchange of currencies, and to (3) neither an initial exchange nor re-exchange, but only payment of the difference as described above. Today all three types of structures are used.

ACCOUNTING FOR SWAPS AND HEDGING

The accounting implications of swaps are considered in detail in Chapter 8. At this stage in the book, however, it is worthwhile considering the general accounting implications and the hedging effect of swaps.

There are many ways in which swaps can be accounted for, and at the time of writing, there is little guidance on this subject by the various accounting bodies. Generally speaking, if the nature of an asset or liability is changed through the use of a swap, one looks at the underlying economic significance of the transaction. If a company transforms a floating rate dollar liability into a simulated fixed rate Swiss franc liability by use of a currency swap, then the resulting simulated liability is what should be accounted for.

The following is a suggested method of accounting for swaps.

General Motors (GM) and Imperial Chemical Industries (ICI) enter into a currency exchange agreement with one another whereby GM initially delivers $10,000,000 to ICI in exchange for ICI delivering £5,000,000 to GM. At maturity of the agreement (eg, five years), both GM and ICI agree to re-exchange currencies in the original equivalent amounts. Initially both GM and ICI lend the proceeds to their foreign subsidiaries. How does GM account for the above transaction?

Suggested solutions

Journal entries	DR $	CR $
1. Currency Exchange ICI	10,000,000	
Cash at Bank ($)		10,000,000
Payment of $ to ICI		
2. Cash at Bank (£)	10,000,000	
Currency Exchange ICI		10,000,000
Receipt from ICI £5,000,000		
@ £1 = US$ 2		
3. GM UK	10,000,000	
Cash at Bank (£)		10,000,000
Loan to UK subsidiary		

GM US Books
(in dollars)

DR	*Cash at Bank ($)*		CR	
		1. CEA − ICI	10,000,000	

DR	*Currency Exchange ICI*		CR	
1. Cash at Bank	$10,000,000	2. Cash at Bank (£)	10,000,000	

DR	*Cash at Bank (£)*		CR	
2. CEA ICI	10,000,000	3. GM UK	10,000,000	

DR	*GM UK*		CR	
3. Cash at Bank (£)	10,000,000			

Under the swap agreement all that happens initially is that there is a reduction in GM's dollar cash and an increase in its sterling cash which it pays away to its UK subsidiary.

Year end

Assuming that GM (US) made a sterling loan to its UK subsidiary and the dollar had appreciated so that £1 = $1, at year end GM would have a translation loss on its inter-company loan of $5,000,000.

However, there would be a corresponding revaluation profit on the swap agreement which would offset the translation loss. How does GM Account for the above?

Suggested solution

The journal entries accounting for the above would be as follows:

	$ DR	$ CR
Translation losses	5,000,000	
GM (UK)		
Translation loss on sterling		5,000,000
loan to GM (UK)		
Deferred Assets	5,000,000	
Translation losses		5,000,000
Revaluation of GM/ICI		
currency exchange agreement		

GM US Books
(in dollars)

DR		GM (UK)		CR
Balance b/d	10,000,000	1. Translation losses		5,000,000
		Balance c/d		5,000,000
	10,000,000			10,000,000
Balance b/d	5,000,000			

DR		*Translation Losses*		CR
1. GM (UK)	5,000,000	2. Deferred assets		5,000,000

DR		*Deferred Assets*		CR
2. Translation losses	5,000,000			

CHAPTER 3

Discounted cash flows and yields to maturity

REVIEW OF DISCOUNTED CASH FLOW PRINCIPLES

The basic concepts surrounding swaps have now been covered. Before we proceed to examine each type of swap in detail, it is essential to understand the principles associated with discounted cash flow techniques and how they relate to determining an entity's cost of funds or return on assets.

Because the swap product essentially arbitrages different capital markets round the world, it is also most important to understand that different countries use different methods for calculating yields relating to the cost of borrowing or return on investments.

This chapter reviews discounted cash flow ('DCF') techniques; the methods used in various countries to calculate yields and the difference between these methods; how DCF theory relates to investments and compares internal rate of return with yield to maturity; and the logic behind the calculation of forward exchange rates.

Calculation of discount factor

First, it is useful to discuss the basic concepts of determining discount factors.

Q. What is the discount factor for 8%?

A. Assume one invests $100 at 8% for 1 year:
Cash flow would be as follows:

Period	Cash flow ($)
0 (cost of investment)	-100
1 (interest)	$+8$
1 (principal)	$+100$
	$+108$

The discount factor ('DF') is the rate by which one must multiply 108 to get 100.

$$\text{ie} \qquad \text{DF} \times 108 = 100$$
$$\text{therefore,} \quad \text{DF} \quad = \frac{100}{108}$$
$$\text{DF} \quad = 0.925926$$

If $100 were invested on a compound interest basis for two years at 8%, in two years' time the following would be received:

1st year	2nd year
(a)	(b)
(a) $= 100 \times 1.08$	(b) $=$ (a) $\times 1.08$
	or $(100 \times 1.08) \times 1.08$
(a) $= 108$	(b) $= 116.64$

So the discount factor is calculated as follows:

$$DF \times (100 \times 1.08) \times 1.08 = 100$$

$$DF = \frac{100}{100 \, (1.08)^2}$$

$$DF = 0.857339$$

If invested for 3 years, one would expect to receive the following

1st year	2nd year	3rd year
(a)	(b)	(c)
(a) = 100 × 1.08	(b) = 100 × 1.08 × 1.08	(c) = 100 × 1.08 × 1.08 × 1.08
	or 100 × $(1.08)^2$	or 100 × $(1.03)^3$
		(c) = 125.97

Again, the discount factor is calculated as follows:

$$DF \times 100 \, (1.08)^3 = 100$$

$$DF = \frac{100}{100 \, (1.08)^3}$$

$$DF \text{ (simplified to)} = \frac{1}{(1.08)^3}$$

$$DF = 0.793832$$

Worded another way, if one invested $79.3832 today, and in three years' time received $100, the return on investment (compound interest) would be 8% per annum.

Discount factors can be reduced to a formula as follows:

$$\text{Discount factor} = \frac{1}{[1 + (\text{Int}/100)]^n}$$

where n = number of periods or years
Int = interest rate %

Q. In summary what does all the foregoing mean?
A. Taking as an example a three year bond purchased at 100 paying interest annually at 8% (or $8) and redeemed at 100 at the end of the third year, a European would say it yields 8% pa.

The following are the cash flow and the pre-calculated discount factors, which when multiplied together gives the present value.

Year	(i) Cash Flow	(ii) Discount Factor	(iii) Present Value (PV) (i) × (ii)
1	8	0.925926	7.41
2	8	0.857339	6.86
3	8	0.793832	6.35
3 Principal { 100		0.793832	79.38
Original cost of investment – PV			$100.00

From the above we can deduce or redefine the yield or discount rate as the rate of interest which, when applied to the future cash flows, discount those amounts such that when added together they equal the initial cost of the investment, ie, the present value.

Before we consider yields to maturity on discount bonds and all-in cost calculations for bond issues it is necessary to point out that the reciprocal of a discount factor equals the compound factor. If we refer to the discount factor for 8% for 1 year, ie 0.925926, we can see that, if we divide 1 by this factor, the answer is 1.08 (or 8%):

$$\text{Compound factor} = \frac{1}{\text{Discount factor}}$$

$$= \frac{1}{0.925926}$$

$$= 1.08$$

COMPARISON OF YIELDS CALCULATION PRINCIPLES

Switzerland, Holland, Belgium, Germany and France (ie, Western Europe) use the foregoing method for calculating yields, which method is also used to calculate yields on all Eurobond issues. The following is the formal definition of maturity yield as issued by the Association of International Bond Dealers (AIBD) for Eurobonds which involve annual payments:

'*Rule 803*

1. The standard AIBD method of calculating maturity yields shall be based on the definition of annual compounding, ie a bond with a 7% coupon, paying annually, priced at 100%, yields 7% per annum and the same bond paying interest semi-annually yields more.

2. A member of the AIBD calculating maturity yields by a method other than the one described above shall state exactly what method has been used for the calculation.'

Domestic US and UK bond issues use a somewhat different method. The difference between the methods relates to the expectation of how many times a year one expects to receive interest. In Europe interest is usually paid annually, while in the US and UK it is paid semi-annually. The US consequently uses semi-annual compounding assumptions for calculating yields, while Europe uses annual compounding.

There are three main methods for calculating yields as follows:

1. Annual coupon   – annual compounding (Euro basis)
2. Semi-annual coupon – semi-annual compounding (US basis)
3. Annual coupon   – semi-annual compounding (Eurobond yields on US basis).

Comparisons of European and US yields calculations

The following example illustrates the difference between European (annual compounding) and US (semi-annual compounding) yields by considering a bond purchased for $100, with an interest rate of 10% payable annually and redeemable at the end of one year at a price of $100. The difference centres entirely round the investor's expectation of whether he should receive his interest payment annually or semi-annually.

European

	$
Principal	100
Theoretical interest due based on yield of 10% payable at end of year	10
Principal + theoretical interest	110
Less: actual interest received	10
Principal	100

US

	$
Principal	100
Theoretical interest due based on yield on 10% payable semi-annually	5
Principal + theoretical interest	105
Actual interest paid semi-annually	0
Principal + theoretical interest	105
Theoretical interest due on new amount of $105 based on yield of 10% payable semi-annually*	5.25
Principal + theoretical interest	110.25
Less: actual interest received	10.00
Principal plus unpaid interest	100.25

To have a 10% yield under the US method, a Eurobond with interest/ coupon payable *annually* and redeemable at par after one year, the interest payment would have to be 10.25% or $10.25.

Compounding and payment frequency

We thus have two methods of calculating yields, ie annual and semi-annual compounding, which can be applied to bonds with varying frequencies of payment of interest, ie annually or semi-annually.

The following example gives three yields which are all correct depending on whether one is using annual or semi-annual compounding, or whether the interest is actually paid annually or semi-annually. The proof of whether the yield is correct, based on the various assumptions, lies in examining the cash flows, as at maturity after the payment of interest the future value should always be 100%.

---

* Because interest is expected to be paid semi-annually, at the end of 6 months when the investor does not receive any interest, he capitalises this amount by adding it to the principal (5 + 100 = 105). Consequently for the next 6 months he expects interest on the new capital amount (ie $105 @ 10% for 6 months = $5.25).

Example

Current price	$85	(PV)
Years to maturity	3	(n)
Coupon/interest rate	8%	(PMT)
Future value	$100	(FV)

Yield to maturity
  Case 1
  — annual coupon,
      annual compounding   14.517%   (i)
  Case 2
  — semi-annual coupon,
      semi-annual compounding   14.326%   (i)
  Case 3
  — annual coupon, semi-
      annual compounding   14.025%   (i)

Key

PV	=	Present value (cost)
n	=	Number of years to maturity
PMT	=	Interest rate or coupon
FV	=	Future value (redemption value)
i	=	Yield to maturity

CASE 1

Annual coupon/annual compounding*

Bond particulars		Equivalent cash flows	
		Yr	$
PV	= $ 85	0	− 85
n	= 3	1	+ 8
PMT	= $ 8	2	+ 8
FV	= $100	3	+ 8
i	= 14.517%	3	+ 100

Proof of yield calculations

(1) PV $	(2) PV × i $	(3) PMT $	(4) (1)+(2)−(3) $
85	12.34	8	89.34
89.34	12.97	8	94.31
94.31	13.69	8	100.00

* Note: interest paid annually and expected annually.

CASE 2

Semi-annual coupon/semi-annual compounding*

Bond particulars		Equivalent cash flows	
		Yr	$
PV	= $ 85	0 −	85
n	= 6	$\frac{1}{2}$ +	4
PMT	= $ 4	1 +	4
FV	= $100	$1\frac{1}{2}$+	4
i	= 7.163%	2 +	4
	× 2	$2\frac{1}{2}$+	4
	= 14.326%	3 +	4
		3 +	100

Proof of yield calculations

(1) PV $	(2) PV × (i/2) $	(3) PMT $	(4) (1)+(2)−(3) $	(5) (4) × (i/2) $	(6) PMT $	(7) (4)+(5)−(6) $
85	6.09	4	87.09	6.24	4	89.33
89.33	6.40	4	91.73	6.57	4	94.30
94.30	6.75	4	97.05	6.95	4	100.00

* Note: interest paid semi-annually and expected semi-annually.

CASE 3

Annual coupon/semi-annual compounding*

Bond particulars		Equivalent cash flows	
		Yr	$
PV	= $ 85	0	− 85
n	= 3	1	+ 8
PMT	= $ 8	2	+ 8
FV	= $100	3	+ 8
i	= 7.0125%	3	+ 100
	× 2		
	= 14.025%		

Proof of yield calculations

(1) PV	(2) PV × (i/2) (7.0125%)	(3) (1)+(2)	(4) (3) × (i/2) (7.0125%)	(5) PMT	(6) (3)+(4)−(5)
$	$	$	$	$	$
85	5.96	90.96	6.38	8	89.34
89.34	6.26	95.60	6.70	8	94.31
94.31	6.61	100.92	7.08	8	100.00

* Note: interest expected semi-annually but only paid annually.

Conversion of Euro to US

Referring to the earlier example, there is a formula for converting Euro yields to US yields and vice versa.

eg   Euro Basis   (Case 1)   14.517%
    US Basis   (Case 3)   14.025%

Formula for conversion

	Euro to US		US to Euro
%	14.517%	%	14.025%
÷ 100	.14517	÷ 100	.14025
+ 1	1.14517	÷ 2	.070126
√	1.070126	+ 1	1.070126
− 1	.070126	( )²	1.41517
* 2	.14025	− 1	.14517
* 100	14.025%	* 100	14.517%

The following is a quick formula for conversion of semi-annual compounding to annual compounding: add the square of half the semi-annual rate to the semi-annual rate to get the annual compounding rate.

$$(\tfrac{1}{2} \times 14.025\%)^2$$
$$= 0.00492$$
$$+ \quad .14025$$
$$\overline{ .14517}$$

APPLYING DCF THEORY

The following hypothetical situation illustrates how the foregoing theory can be applied from a practical point of view.

Example

A man calls on an insurance company and says 'How much would I have to pay as a premium today in order for you to write me an insurance policy under which you would make me the following payments in the future?'

Year	1	2	3	4	5
Amount $'s	80	95	110	60	40

Question

How can the insurance company calculate the amount of premium to charge.

Assumption

1. The insurance company decides to generate the income to meet these future payments by investing in dollar Eurobonds.
2. For simplicity, assume a breakeven situation (ie, exclude insurance company's profit margin) such that the cost of buying the investments will equal the premium to be charged.
3. The insurance company can buy dollar Eurobonds at the following yields:

	Years				
Maturity (n)	1	2	3	4	5
Yield to Maturity (i) (annual compounding)	7%	9%	15%	14%	13%

4. Yields to maturity and amounts in this example have been chosen at random.
5. Tax implications are ignored.

Answer

The approach to solving this problem is to work backwards. We know that the insurance company must generate $40 in year five and that five-year Eurobonds are yielding 13% p.a.

Step 1

The first step is to calculate the nominal amount of a 13% Eurobond the insurance company needs to purchase such that the redemption value plus the accrued interest paid at the end of the fifth year equals 40. This is calculated as follows:

Nominal amount $\div (1 + \text{interest rate}) = $ required amount

or

$$\text{nominal amount} = \$40/1.13$$
$$= \$35.40$$

Interest on the bond would amount to $4.60 per annum ($35.40 × 13% = $4.60).

Step 2

The next step is to calculate the nominal amount of the four-year 14% Eurobond the insurance company must buy to generate $60 at the end of the fourth year. It must be remembered, however, that an allowance must be made for the income received on the already purchased five-year 13% Eurobond of $4.60 which will be received each year from years one to five. The amount the insurance company needs to generate at the end of the fourth year is not $60 but $60 less $4.60. The nominal amount for the four years is then determined similarly to above: ie

$$\text{Nominal amount} = \frac{\$60 - \$4.60}{1.14}$$
$$= \$48.60$$

Step 3

Having determined the nominal amount of bonds the insurance company needs to purchase in years five and four to determine the amount for year three, given three-year Eurobond yields, Step 2 is repeated and so on for year two and year one.

The following table illustrates these steps:

		Yield	Amount of Euro-bond to be purchased Nominal	Interest year					Total	Total
Step	Year	%	$	1	2	3	4	5	interest	cash flow
	1	7	46.64	3.26	5.84	12.86	6.80	4.60	33.36	80.00
	2	9	64.90		5.84	12.86	6.80	4.60	30.10	95.00
3	3	15	85.74			12.86	6.80	4.60	24.26	110.00
2	4	14	48.60				6.80	4.60	11.40	60.00
1	5	13	35.40					4.60	4.60	40.00
			281.28						103.72	375.00

From this we can conclude that the insurance company would have to charge the Policy Holder $281.28 in order to have sufficient capital or funds to buy Eurobond investments which would generate the necessary cash flow to meet the payments under the Policy.

Using the foregoing example provides the opportunity to refer back to theory on calculating discount factors and to show how discount factors and yields to maturity all relate to cash flows. In other words any cash flow can be broken down to principal and interest or related to yields which in turn relate to discounted cash flow theory.

Internal rate of return compared with discount factors

Returning to the above example, the internal rate of return, that is, the rate which discounts all future cash flows to the present value, can be readily calculated (using most financial calculators).

The known facts are:

	$		Steps
Cost of Policy	− 281.28	g	CFO
Payments under Policy			
year 1	80.00	g	CFJ
2	95.00	g	CFJ
3	110.00	g	CFJ
4	60.00	g	CFJ
5	40.00	g	CFJ
Internal Rate of Return or			
Return on Investment	12.7858%	f	IRR

For those who do not have calculators, the IRR of 12.7858% can be calculated and proved long hand. If we refer back to how to calculate a discount rate given a yield or IRR of 12.7858%, we can calculate a discount factor for each of the years which can be applied to the future values (receipts) in order to determine a present value which should sum to $281.28 as follows:

Future cash flow (1)	Discount factor	or		Present value (1) × (2) $
			(2)	
80	$1 \div 1.127858$		.8866	70.93
95	$1 \div (1.127858)^2$		.7861	74.68

110	$1 \div (1.127858)^3$	.6970	76.67
60	$1 \div (1.127858)^4$	.6180	37.08
40	$1 \div (1.127858)^5$	.5479	21.92
			281.28

Internal rate of return compared with yield to maturity

The logic used for explaining the difference between semi-annual and annual compounding, ie, capitalising unearned interest, can also be used to prove this rate of 12.7858% from the investor's point of view (the above rate of return calculated on an annual compounding basis).

If we take the amount that the policy holder pays on day one of $281.28 and inform him the future payments that the insurance company is to make to him of $80, $95, $100 and so on for the next five years is equivalent to a yield of 12.7858%, then this yield, which is the same as the internal rate of return, can be proved as follows.

If the policy holder invests $281.28 at a yield of 12.7858%, at the end of year one he would expect an interest payment of $35.96. However, he is paid $80 and the difference of $44.04 is in effect a reduction of the principal amount of $281.28 to $237.24. Using this approach, if the yield of 12.7858% is correct, the principal amount should reduce to 'Zero' at the end of the fifth year as per the following table:

Year	Original principal	Interest payments $(1) \times 12.7858\%$	Payment to policy holder	Amount of Capital reduction $(3)-(2)$	New capital $(1)-(4)$
	(1)	(2)	(3)	(4)	(5)
	$	$	$	$	$
1	281.28	35.96	80.00	44.04	237.24
2	237.24	30.33	95.00	64.67	172.57
3	172.57	22.07	110.00	87.93	84.64
4	84.64	10.82	60.00	49.18	35.47
5	35.47	4.53	40.00	35.47	NIL

The conclusions from the foregoing are: (1) any cash flow can be generated by acquiring a suitable asset; (2) knowing the basis of compounding, any cash flow can be broken down into principal and interest given the yield to maturity; (3) given the cost of an investment, the basis of compounding and the future cash flows (or income streams) the IRR or yield to the investor (or cost to the borrower) can be calculated; and (4) points 1, 2, and 3 above are all inter-related.

Importance of 'day basis' for interest calculations

There is one other important factor to be introduced into yield calculations and that is the 'day basis' of calculating the amount of interest paid. This is best illustrated by comparing a Eurobond and a bank deposit. If an investor were to invest $100 in a 10% Eurobond redeemable for $100 at the end of one year his cash flow would be as follows:

	Period		$
	0	Cost of investment	−100
	1	Interest	10
	1	Principal	100
			110

His yield to maturity on an annual compounding basis would be 10%.

However if he were to invest $100 in a one-year Eurodollar bank deposit at 10% his yield would be 10.1389% as interest in the bank deposit market is calculated as follows:

$$\frac{\text{principal} \times \text{actual no. of days} \times \text{rate} \,\%}{360}$$

or $\qquad \$100 \times \dfrac{365}{360} \times .10 = \$10.1389$ or 10.1389%

ie, actual number of elapsed days (366 on a leap year) over a base of 360. However, interest on bonds* is effectively calculated on the actual number of days elapsed over the actual number of days as follows:

$$\text{principal} \times \frac{\text{actual no. of days}}{\text{actual no. of days}} \times \text{rate} \,\%$$

or $\qquad \$100 \times \dfrac{365}{365} \times .10 = \$10$

'Day basis' is extremely important in working out yields of US Treasury Bills as prices are quoted on a discount basis and yields calculated on a discount yield basis. These yields need to be converted to a bond equivalent for comparison with the US bond market. The following example illustrates this difference and shows how discount yields can be converted to bond equivalents. (The examples used relate to paper of six months' duration or less.)

Example: calculation of discount rate and bond equivalent on 3 and 6 month treasuries

	3 month	6 month
Value date	Sept 8, 1983	Sept 8, 1983
Price	97.672%	95.248%
Future value	100.00	100.00
Redemption date	Dec 8, 1983	March 8, 1983
Days	Sept 22	Sept 22
	Oct 31	Oct 31
	Nov 30	Nov 30
	Dec 8	Dec 31
	91	Jan 31
		Feb 29
		Mar 8
		182

---

* This is not quite accurate for Eurobonds. Accrued interest for Eurobonds is calculated on the basis of twelve 30-day months over a basis of 360 days ie 360/360. For example January and February both have 30 days for Eurobond interest calculation purposes where as for the deposit market they have 31 and 28 days, respectively.

Calculation of yield	*3 month*	*6 month*
(I) *Discount rate*	$\dfrac{100-97.672}{100}\times\dfrac{360}{91}$ $=9.21\%$	$\dfrac{100-95.248}{100}\times\dfrac{360}{182}$ $=9.40\%$
(II) *Bond equivalent*	$\dfrac{100-97.672}{97.672}\times\dfrac{365}{91}$ $=9.56\%$	$\dfrac{100-95.248}{95.248}\times\dfrac{365}{182}$ $=10.01\%$

Conversion formula

$$\text{discount rate}\times\frac{365}{360}\times\frac{100}{\text{Price}}$$

$$9.21\%\times\frac{365}{360}\times\frac{100}{97.672} \qquad 9.40\%\times\frac{365}{360}\times\frac{100}{95.248}$$
$$=9.56\% \qquad\qquad =10.01\%$$

or

$$\frac{\text{discount rate}}{1-\left(\dfrac{\text{Discount rate}}{100}\times\dfrac{\text{days}}{360}\right)}\times\frac{365}{360}$$

$$\frac{9.21}{1-\left(\dfrac{9.21}{100}\times\dfrac{91}{360}\right)}\times\frac{365}{360} \qquad \frac{9.40}{1-\left(\dfrac{9.40}{100}\times\dfrac{182}{360}\right)}\times\frac{365}{360}$$
$$=9.56\% \qquad\qquad\qquad =10.01\%$$

The following is a list of the more important instruments, frequency of payment and period (days) for interest calculation purposes.

Instrument	Pricing on interest Payment frequency	Day count basis
US Treasury Issues	Discount price	Actual/360
US Treasury Bonds	*Periodic	Actual/Actual
US Treasury Notes	*Periodic	Actual/Actual
Federal National Mortgage Assoc. (FNMA) Debentures	*Periodic	30/360
General National Mortgage Assoc. (GNMA) Bond and Participation Certificates	*Periodic	30/360
Bankers Acceptances (US)	Discount	Actual/360
Certificates of Deposit (US)	Discount at maturity Periodic	Actual/360 30/360
Commercial Paper	Discount at maturity	Actual/360
Corporate Bonds (US)	*Periodic	30/360
Eurobonds	†Periodic	30/360

* Usually semi-annually.
† Usually annually.

EXPLANATION OF CALCULATING FORWARD EXCHANGE RATES

Prior to returning to the swap product, forward foreign exchange rates need to be considered in further detail. This topic was briefly covered in Chapter 2, where it was stated that the forward premium or discount on the forward sale of one currency for another depends on interest differentials prevailing in the interbank deposit market.

Working from the basis that forward rates are effectively breakeven rates (ie, a bank should not be able to profit by borrowing Swiss francs, selling them spot for dollars, placing dollars on deposit and selling forward dollars at maturity for Swiss francs), the following outlines a simple illustration of how a forward rate can be calculated. It must be stressed, however, that markets are not perfect or logical and do not work to set rules. The example is based on compound interest principles and does not allow for other market practices or factors.

Question

Given the following market information, theoretically how would a bank determine the forward exchange rate for selling dollars forward for Swiss francs in three years' time.

Market information

Principal amounts	$	100
	SFr	218
Borrowing rate – 3 years	SFr	5%
Deposit rate – 3 years	$	12%
Spot rate	$1 = SFr 2.18	

Assumption

Assume annual compounding and rate of return unchanged over three years.

Solution

Step 1

Determine the total amount of Swiss francs to be paid and dollars to be received at end of three years as follows:

Borrowing (SFr)					Deposit ($)				
YR	P	*	$(1+i) = P+i$		YR	P	*	$(1+i) = P+i$	
1	218	*	1.05	= A	1	100	*	1.12	= X
2	A	*	1.05	= B	2	X	*	1.12	= Y
3	B	*	1.05	= C	3	Y	*	1.12	= Z
			or SFr 252.36					or $'s 140.49	

P   = Principal (SFr 218, $100)
$(1+i)$ = 1 plus the interest rate (ie SFr $1+.05$, $1 + .12$)
$P+i$ = Principal plus capitalised interest (ie new principal)
C   = SFr Principal plus capitalised interest at end or third year

Z   = Dollar Principal plus capitalised interest at end or third year
*   = Multiply

Step 2

Determine forward rate by dividing total amounts of Swiss francs, C, by total amount of dollars, Z, as determined under step 1 above.

$$\text{Forward rate} = C/Z$$
$$\text{or } \$1 = \text{SFr } 1.7963$$

The above longhand method of calculating the forward rate can be reduced to the following formula:

$$\text{Forward rate} = \text{Spot} * \frac{(1 + \text{SFr\%})^n}{(1 + \$\%)^n}$$

Where n   = number of years

or as per the above example:

$$\text{Forward rate} = 2.18 * \frac{(1.05)^3}{(1.12)^3}$$
$$= 1.7963$$

CHAPTER 4

The structure of swaps

Swaps can be grouped into five main categories:

   (i) interest rate or coupon swaps, ie, same currency floating to fixed swaps;

  (ii) cross-currency fixed-to-fixed swaps;

 (iii) cross-currency fixed-to-floating swaps;

 (iv) same currency floating-to-floating swaps;

  (v) cross-currency floating-to-floating swaps.

It is also possible to have a series of transactions involving more than one of the above types of swap. This chapter will discuss general terms of swaps and also each of the foregoing types on an individual basis. Different approaches will be used in discussing different categories as an illustration of alternative ways of studying the swap product.

GENERAL TERMS AND CONDITIONS

Swap financings require at least two parties mutually agreeing to terms and conditions. Consequently, they can be as flexible as is required by the commercial needs of the parties involved. Exchange control and other government regulations, including taxation, have to be considered.

The following is a general guide to terms and conditions that apply to most interest and currency swap financings.

Amount: Typical amounts are $10,000,000 to $100,000,000 or more, or the equivalent in other currencies (most contracts tend to be in multiples of $25,000,000).

Currencies: Provided structures can be devised to overcome restrictive regulations (if any), swaps can be arranged between any currencies. The most common currencies are: dollars, Canadian dollars, pounds sterling, Deutschemarks, Swiss francs, Japanese yen and Dutch guilders, although swaps have also been arranged in other currencies such as Australian dollars, French francs, Belgian francs and European Currency Units.

Maturities: Swap financings tend to be medium to long term, generally three to ten years (though longer is possible) and are usually entered into when no forward foreign market exists for medium to long-term maturities between the respective currencies.

Amortization:

Swap contracts usually involve notional principal amounts repayable on a single maturity date ('bullet' maturity). Amortizing provisions are possible provided a suitable counterparty can be found.

Notional interest:
(pricing/fee:)

Interest swaps

For interest rate swaps pricing is determined by market conditions relating to fixed rate borrowing costs, floating-rate cost objectives and credit ratings.

Currency swaps
For currency swaps, pricing is subject to negotiation but generally will reflect interest differentials prevailing between currencies involved as determined by yields on governmental bonds for the maturity involved.

Interest differentials are not, however, the only determining factor. Other considerations, such as governmental policy, liquidity, demand and devaluation expectations and credit rating also apply.

The fee reflecting interest differentials in a currency swap can be taken into account by way of an annual payment from one party to another, by adjusting the future exchange rate or by both parties making gross notional interest payments. This fee is usually paid by the forward seller of the higher yielding currency.

Future obligations:

Interest swaps
In the case of interest rate swaps, this will involve the sale of amounts calculated by reference to a floating rate of interest and a fixed rate of interest, both sales being contingent upon one another.

Currency swaps
Swap contracts represent obligations by both parties to deliver pre-determined amounts of currencies to one another in the future. Non-performance by one party to deliver 'negates' the obligation of the other party to deliver. However, the injured party retains the right to claim for damages to the extent it suffers losses through non-performance.

Acceleration:

Swap agreements usually contain acceleration provisions in the event of certain occurrences in respect of either party including: standard events of default, non-payment of annual fee or non-performance of any obligation under the agreement.

Arrangement fee:

Usually between $\frac{1}{4}$ to $\frac{1}{2}$ percent of the amount involved payable on the signing of the contract to the arranger.

Intermediary fee: From .0010 to .0025 (ie, 10 to 25 basis points) per annum, depending on type of swap credit risk, for a bank to act as intermediary.

Other expenses: The arranger of swaps will expect to be reimbursed for all out-of-pocket expenses including legal fees incurred in relation to the preparation, execution and delivery of the swap agreement.

Documentation: Standard documents which are now in force for swap contracts are usually between six to fifteen pages, or longer depending upon the complexity of the transaction involved.

Governing law: Governing law will depend on the domicile of the parties involved, reputations of the legal jurisdictions with respect to international financial matters and the place of payments – generally New York or England.

   Examples of structures are as follows.

Cross-border swap: a swap contract written by two parties with different domiciles.

Domestic swap: a swap contract written between two parties in the same domicile.

Parallel loan: a transaction where two parties simultaneously make loans for the same value to one another's foreign subsidiary, such that each loan does not involve a cross-border movement of currency.

Back-to-back loan: a transaction similar to a cross-border swap except that two cross-border loans (usually parent-to-parent) are involved for the respective currencies, represented by either separate loan documentation or by one document.

Simulated currency   a simulated currency loan in one currency, with the
loan: terms of the loan indexed to another currency. The lender transfers the exchange exposure to the borrower, who assumes the exchange risk but in return has the benefit of the term and structure of interest payments in his domestic currency.

                    *   *   *   *   *

In discussing the five basic forms of swap mentioned at the beginning of this chapter, we will assume the following structure. Two unrelated entities will have, either at or before the date of the swap, independently incurred interest-bearing liabilities or acquired assets on which they require a return. The liabilities/assets are in the same or different currencies and usually bear interest or require a return calculated on a different basis. The entities will agree to make payments to each other (either directly or through an intermediary) with the effect that each party pays to the other the direct liability incurred by, or a return on the asset required by, the other.

More simply worded, a swap is an agreement whereby two parties, either directly or through a bank intermediary, agree to service each other's debt. Of course, liabilities incurred do not have to match exactly; only the portion of the liabilities covered by the swap need match. In addition, parties may accept mismatches if the terms otherwise compensate.

INTEREST RATE OR COUPON SWAP: SAME CURRENCY FLOATING-TO-FIXED SWAPS

The word 'coupon' usually relates to bearer bonds with interest certificates attached. On each interest payment date a coupon is cut from the bearer bond and presented to the paying agent for payment. In a coupon swap, the parties will typically have borrowed identical principal amounts for the same period, one borrowing on a fixed-rate basis and the other borrowing on a floating-rate basis. Through the swap, each party pays to the other an amount calculated by reference to the recipient's borrowing basis.

There are three main reasons for the rapid development of coupon swaps. First, as mentioned above, central bank regulations forced banks to fund term floating-rate assets with term liabilities as opposed to short-term deposits.

The second is the exploitation of a credit anomaly: the spread (margin) differentials which exist between the public capital market and the bank credit market. The following schedule illustrates credit differences existing at the time of writing between the dollar denominated Eurobond capital market and the Eurodollar syndicated bank loan market.

Borrower	Term (years)	Capital Market %	Bank Market %
Lesser credit	5−7	13.0	LIBOR $+\frac{1}{2}$
Strong credit	5−7	11.5	LIBOR $+\frac{1}{4}$
Credit spread		1.5	0.25

Thus, banks are quite willing to lend lesser credits floating-rate finance on a term basis, but the problem for banks in lending fixed-rate finance has been their inability to fund themselves on a long-term fixed-rate basis. Many of these lesser credits cannot raise finance by issuing fixed-rate bonds, or can only do so at an unacceptably high cost. The advent of the interest rate or coupon swap has corrected this mismatch. Now it has become regular practice for strong borrowers to borrow on a fixed-rate basis, such as through a public Eurobond issue, and turn such borrowing into cheap floating-rate finance via a swap. Conversely, a lesser credit will borrow medium-term finance on a floating-rate basis and transform this funding to a fixed-rate basis by entering into an interest rate swap with a fixed-rate issuer (or through an intermediary bank).

The third reason, which is related to the second, and probably the over-riding consideration, is the one of 'cost of funds'. Banks, particularly the non-dollar based banks, realised that, by exploiting the above credit anomaly, they could raise floating-rate dollars through a swap related bond issue more cheaply than through conventional means such as bank deposits, certificates of deposit, floating-rate CD's and floating-rate notes. Obviously, a bank which launches a fixed-rate Eurobond issue and turns it into a simulated floating-rate liability via a coupon or interest rate swap must also conclude that the cost saving outweighs the additional risks such as the credit risk of its counterparty and possible impairment of its future ability to issue fixed-rate debt.

A good example is the already mentioned Deutsche Bank Luxembourg swap. In December 1982, Deutsche Bank Luxembourg issued a $110 million 11% Eurobond issue due 1989, and reportedly converted this obligation into a simulated floating-rate obligation at an all-in cost (ie after issue expenses) at $\frac{1}{4}$% under LIBOR. This transaction can be illustrated as follows:

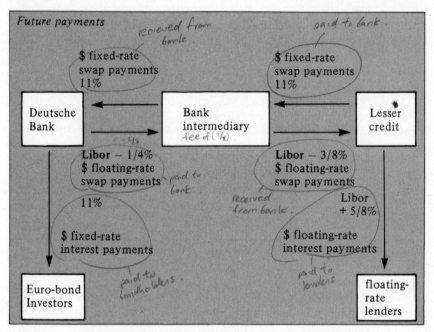

(Note: It is assumed from market 'gossip' that the intermediary received $\frac{1}{8}$% for acting as principal and that the lesser credit paid a margin of $\frac{5}{8}$% over LIBOR for its floating-rate debt; this may or may not reflect actual margins.)

Simulated cost of funds

Mathematically it is easy to see what it cost Deutsche Bank and the lesser credit to raise simulated floating- and fixed-rate debt, respectively, by looking at the balance or net interest paid column in the table entitled 'Cash Flow Schedule'. In Deutsche's case, the cost is obviously LIBOR $-\frac{1}{4}$%, while the lesser credit must pay 1.0% per annum payable semi-annually (ie $\frac{5}{8}$% + $\frac{3}{8}$%) plus 11% annually, which translates into a cost on an annual compounding basis of 12.03%.

CASH FLOW SCHEDULE

| | Deutsche Bank | | | | Lesser credit | | | |
| | | Swap | | | | Swap | | |
Date	Schedule A Payments to Bondholders	Schedule B Payments to Intermediary	Schedule C Receipts from Intermediary	Balance Net Interest Paid	Schedule D Payments to Syndicate of Banks	Schedule E Payments to Intermediary	Schedule F Receipts from Intermediary	Balance Net Interest Paid
	%	%	%	%	%	%	%	%
6.83	—	LIBOR $-\frac{1}{4}$	—	LIBOR $-\frac{1}{4}$	LIBOR $+\frac{5}{8}$	—	LIBOR $-\frac{3}{8}$	0.5
12.83	11.00	LIBOR $-\frac{1}{4}$	11.00	LIBOR $-\frac{1}{4}$	LIBOR $+\frac{5}{8}$	11.00	LIBOR $-\frac{3}{8}$	11.5
6.84	—	LIBOR $-\frac{1}{4}$	—	LIBOR $-\frac{1}{4}$	LIBOR $+\frac{5}{8}$	—	LIBOR $-\frac{3}{8}$	0.5
12.84	11.00	LIBOR $-\frac{1}{4}$	11.00	LIBOR $-\frac{1}{4}$	LIBOR $+\frac{5}{8}$	11.00	LIBOR $-\frac{3}{8}$	11.5
6.85	—	LIBOR $-\frac{1}{4}$	—	LIBOR $-\frac{1}{4}$	LIBOR $+\frac{5}{8}$	—	LIBOR $-\frac{3}{8}$	0.5
12.85	11.00	LIBOR $-\frac{1}{4}$	11.00	LIBOR $-\frac{1}{4}$	LIBOR $+\frac{5}{8}$	11.00	LIBOR $-\frac{3}{8}$	11.5
6.86	—	LIBOR $-\frac{1}{4}$	—	LIBOR $-\frac{1}{4}$	LIBOR $+\frac{5}{8}$	—	LIBOR $-\frac{3}{8}$	0.5
12.86	11.00	LIBOR $-\frac{1}{4}$	11.00	LIBOR $-\frac{1}{4}$	LIBOR $+\frac{5}{8}$	11.00	LIBOR $-\frac{3}{8}$	11.5
6.87	—	LIBOR $-\frac{1}{4}$	—	LIBOR $-\frac{1}{4}$	LIBOR $+\frac{5}{8}$	—	LIBOR $-\frac{3}{8}$	0.5
12.87	11.00	LIBOR $-\frac{1}{4}$	11.00	LIBOR $-\frac{1}{4}$	LIBOR $+\frac{5}{8}$	11.00	LIBOR $-\frac{3}{8}$	11.5
6.88	—	LIBOR $-\frac{1}{4}$	—	LIBOR $-\frac{1}{4}$	LIBOR $+\frac{5}{8}$	—	LIBOR $-\frac{3}{8}$	0.5
12.88	11.00	LIBOR $-\frac{1}{4}$	11.00	LIBOR $-\frac{1}{4}$	LIBOR $+\frac{5}{8}$	11.00	LIBOR $-\frac{3}{8}$	11.5
6.89	—	LIBOR $-\frac{1}{4}$	—	LIBOR $-\frac{1}{4}$	LIBOR $+\frac{5}{8}$	—	LIBOR $-\frac{3}{8}$	0.5
12.89	11.00	LIBOR $-\frac{1}{4}$	11.00	LIBOR $-\frac{1}{4}$	LIBOR $+\frac{5}{8}$	11.00	LIBOR $-\frac{3}{8}$	11.5
12.89	100.00			100.00				100.00

Conclusion

Swaps may seem to be complicated but when reduced to cash flows it can be seen that conceptually they are simple and the result easily determined as the net payments or receipt column represents a company's cost of funds or return on assets. This statement applies to all forms of swap.

Calculation format

Following is a format for calculating costs for a transaction involving a bond issue and a new syndicated loan based on the following information.

Debt	*Bond issue*	*Syndicated loan*
Borrower:	Strong credit	Lesser credit
Amount	$50 million	$50 million
Issue price	100%	100%
Coupon/interest	11% payable annually	LIBOR + $\frac{5}{8}$% payable semi-annually
Redemption	At maturity	At maturity
Maturity	7 years	7 years
Commission/fees	2%	$\frac{1}{2}$%

Swap (with intermediary):		
Parties	Strong credit	Lesser credit
Notional principal amount	$50 million	$50 million
Interest/coupon sold	LIBOR $-\frac{1}{2}$% payable semi-annually	11.485% payable annually
Interest/coupon purchased	11.485% payable annually	LIBOR $-\frac{1}{2}$% payable semi-annually
Maturity	7 years	7 years
Arrangement fee	$\frac{1}{4}$%	$\frac{1}{4}$%

Other information:		
Swap intermediary Fee		$\frac{1}{8}$% per annum paid semi-annually

	Front end %	Semi-annual %	Annual %	Annual equivalent %
Strong credit				
Payments:				
Bonds				
Commissions	2.000			0.430
Interest			11.000	11.000
				11.430
Swaps				
Fees	0.250			.055
Interest		LIBOR $-\frac{1}{2}$		
		LIBOR $-\frac{1}{2}$		11.485
Receipts:				
Swap				
Interest				11.485
All-In-Cost		LIBOR $-\frac{1}{2}$		Nil

	Front end %	Semi-annual %	Annual %	Annual equivalent %
Lesser credit				
Payments:				
Syndicated Loan				
Commission	0.500			0.108
Interest		LIBOR $+\frac{5}{8}$		
Swap				
Commission	0.250			0.055
Annual Fee		$\frac{1}{8}$		
Interest				11.485
		LIBOR $+\frac{3}{4}$		11.648
Receipts:				
Swap				
Interest		LIBOR $-\frac{1}{2}$		
Net Payment		1.250		
Conversion				
an to s-an eq		11.327		(11.648)
All-In- Cost		*12.577		Nil
(on s-an				
compounding				
basis)				

Note: Annual equivalent 12.97%

an = Annual
s-an = Semi-annual
eq = Equivalent

CROSS-CURRENCY FIXED-TO-FIXED SWAP

In a cross-currency fixed-to-fixed swap, the parties will typically have borrowed principal amounts in different currencies but which are initially the equivalent of each other at spot rates, each bearing interest on a fixed-rate basis. Through the swap, each party pays the other an amount calculated by reference to the recipient's interest rate, coupled with the payment of the recipient's principal amount at maturity.

Case Study: 1

The following is a hypothetical case study of a fixed-to-fixed cross-currency debt swap which illustrates how an anomaly can be exploited to the benefit of both parties. It involves a hypothetical debt swap between Phillip Morris ('PM') and World Bank ('WB'), under which PM would raise Swiss francs and WB dollars. The hypothetical situation, based on circumstances and market conditions prevailing at the time of writing, is as follows.

PM is a large industrial company in the US, whose outstanding US debt is currently A-rated by Standard and Poors (AAA being the highest rating). However, PM can borrow Swiss francs on effectively AAA terms. In Switzerland PM is well known and regarded as a 'blue chip' company, partly because PM has launched a number of successful Swiss franc bond issues, especially convertible bond issues, in the past. It is also so regarded because good quality US industrial paper is scarce in Switzerland. Also adding to PM's appeal is that the Swiss, in addition to their own country, regard America as a safe country in which to invest. This benefits all potential American borrowers in the Swiss franc capital market. On the other hand,

PM only borrows on A rated terms in the US, where there is no scarcity of A rated (ie, less favoured) industrial paper. This is the first anomaly.

Alternatively, WB is AAA rated in the US, but has borrowed for many years in the Swiss capital market and to such an extent that many Swiss investors are long of WB paper. The Swiss investor who is not quite saturated is starting to demand a premium for buying WB paper, a second anomaly. WB, however, has a declared policy of borrowing low interest rate currencies, such as the Swiss franc, Deutschemark and yen, and has a need for Swiss franc debt in excess of what the Swiss franc capital market can stand a third anomaly.

The advent of the currency swap has been a boon for WB in that it can utilise its surplus dollar borrowing ability, coupled with its ability to borrow on AAA terms, to generate simulated Swiss franc debt by entering into a currency exchange swap agreement with borrowers who can borrow in the Swiss capital market but who would prefer fixed-rate dollar debt.

Consequently an opportunity would exist for WB and PM enter into a currency swap, under which WB would agree to service PM's Swiss franc borrowing costs, in return for PM servicing WB's dollar borrowing costs.

The case study has been set out on a question and answer basis to illustrate the steps involved in working out each party's costs in generating simulated fixed-rate finance through the swap. It also assumes that the reader has access to a calculator programmed to calculate bond yields on an annual compounding basis, or a set of bond yield tables.

Given information

1. PM and WB are prepared to enter into a cross-currency fixed-to-fixed debt swap.

2. PM can borrow Swiss francs on the following terms:

amount:	SFr 100 million
interest rate (coupon):	$5\frac{3}{8}\%$, payable annually
maturity:	8 years
redemption:	at maturity
issuing costs:	3.25%

3. WB has existing dollar debt with a remaining life of 8 years, which it borrowed at an all-in cost of 11.9% on an annual compounding basis.

4. WB is prepared to swap out of its dollar debt into a simulated Swiss franc obligation at an all-in cost of Swiss francs 5.75% on an annual compounding basis (no allowance has been made in this case study for paying agency fees in connection with the payments of principal and interest).

5. The assumed exchange rate prevailing at the time of entering into the swap is $1 = SFr 2.10.

Questions

1. What is PM's all-in Swiss franc borrowing cost on an annual compounding basis? Also calculate the cost on a semi-annual compounding basis.

2. What is PM's all-in cost of simulating fixed-rate dollar debt (under the swap WB would agree to service PM's principal and interest payments under its Swiss franc debt obligation, in return for PM similarly servicing WB's dollar debt obligation)?

3. Construct a cash flow diagram showing the cash flows involved, and list the cash flows under PM's Swiss franc bond issue and the swap with WB.

Assumptions

1. PM sells the net proceeds of its Swiss franc bond issue for dollars through the foreign exchange market at the prevailing spot dollar/Swiss franc rate, ie $1 = SFr 2.10.

2. Conversely WB sells dollars for Swiss francs, also through the foreign exchange market, at the same rate.

Solution

Q. 1. Calculation of PM's Swiss franc borrowing cost

	Swiss franc amount of issue		
	Swiss francs millions	%	
Amount of issue	100.000	100.00	
less: issue costs	3.250	3.25	
Net proceeds	96.750	96.75	(PV)
Interest (coupon) payable annually	5.375	5.375	(PMT)
Years to maturity		8	(n)
Redemption value	100.000	100.00	(FV)

Given the above information it is possible to calculate PM's all-in cost of borrowing SFr's:

Yield to maturity (all-in cost)	(i)
annual compounding basis	5.90%
semi-annual compounding basis	5.81%

This all-in cost of 5.90% represents the discount rate which when applied to eight annual payments of interest of 5.375% and the repayment of principal of 100% in year eight gives a present value of 96.75%.

Key: PV = present value of net proceeds
PMT = interest or coupon payments
n   = number of years to maturity
FV = redemption value of bond issue
i   = yield to maturity

Note: these abbreviations are used throughout the rest of the case studies.

Q. 2. What is PM's all-in cost of simulating fixed-rate dollar debt?

The starting point is to determine the nominal dollar value of WB's dollar debt which would be subject to the swap. This is done as follows.

Step 1

Determine the present value of the future interest and principal payments to be made by PM to the Swiss franc bond holders by discounting these future payments at WB's target all-in Swiss franc borrowing cost of 5.75% which we know from the given information is all that WB is prepared to pay:

PM's annual (coupon) payment	5.375%	(PMT)
years to maturity	8	(n)
redemption value	100%	(FV)
WB's all-in cost	5.75%	(i)
present value	97.65%	(PV)
or Swiss francs	97,648,111	

Step 2

Convert the Swiss franc present value determined in step 1 above to dollars using the prevailing exchange rate of $1 = SFr 2.10. This determines the nominal amount of WB's outstanding dollar debt to be converted into simulated Swiss francs under the currency swap agreement.

Present value	SFr 97,648,111
Exchange rate	$1 = SFr 2.10
Nominal dollar equivalent	$46,499,100

Step 3

Having determined the nominal dollar value of WB's dollar debt to be converted, given WB's borrowing cost of 11.9% annual compounding, the next step is to determine the annual amount which needs to be paid to WB by PM, in order for WB to service the future interest and principal payments on the nominal amount of its debt, as determined under 2 above, of $46,499,100.

Interest (coupon) payments:

nominal amount of WB's dollar debt	$46,499,100
WB's interest cost	11.9%
annual payment	$ 5,533,393
principal payment (redemption value)	$46,499,100

We have now established the dollar amounts PM will have to sell to WB under the swap.

Step 4

Determine the dollar amount PM receives by selling the Swiss franc proceeds of its bond issue through the foreign exchange market:

net proceeds of issue	SFr 96,750,000
exchange rate	$1 = SFr 2.10
US dollar equivalent	$46,071,429

This dollar amount is the present value (PV) of PM's simulated fixed-rate dollar debt.

Step 5

It is now possible to calculate PM's all-in cost of simulating fixed-rate dollar debt, based on the following previously determined information:

	amount	%
PM's simulated fixed-rate debt terms:		
(a) present value of dollar simulated fixed-rate debt, as per 4 above	$46,071,429	99.08% (PV)
(b) annual dollar interest payments (coupon) to be made to WB, as per 3 above	$ 5,533,393	11.9 % (PMT)
(c) years to maturity (remaining life), as per given information		8 (n)
(d) the future value of PM's simulated fixed-rate dollar debt or the amount of dollar principal to be paid to WB under the swap, as per 2 above	$46,499,100	100.0 % (PV)
(e) all-in cost of PM's simulated fixed-rate dollar debt		12.09% (i)

Summary of the logic

The number of Swiss francs PM needs to buy from WB is already known, given the terms of PM's Swiss franc issue. The question becomes how many dollars does PM have to sell to WB in return for buying the required amount of Swiss francs. The question for WB then becomes how much dollar debt can be serviced by the dollars purchased from PM. The way this is done is by discounting PM's future Swiss franc interest and principal payments at WB's target Swiss franc borrowing cost of 5.75% to determine a PV. This Swiss franc PV is converted to dollars at the current spot exchange rate. This becomes the principal dollar amount of WB's debt. PM then pays the dollar interest on WB dollar debt to WB each year and the principal amount at maturity. After converting the net proceeds of PM's Swiss franc issue to dollars, PM's simulated dollar borrowing costs can be determined.

Q. 3. Future payments

Case Study: 2

The next hypothetical case study (see diagram on p. 46) deals with a fixed-rate assets/liability swap, and again illustrates how an anomaly can be exploited to the benefit of both parties.

The situation, based on circumstances and market conditions prevailing at the time of writing, is as follows.

A Japanese government borrower is interested in raising fixed-rate dollar debt in the US by way of a domestic fixed-rate dollar bond offering (a yankee bond issue). It would prefer to raise yen debt directly in Japan, but is being encouraged by the Ministry of Finance to raise finance externally.

The Ministry of Finance is at the same time encouraging Japanese investors to diversify their portfolios by buying foreign assets. The Japanese investor, however, does not want the foreign currency exposure associated with this, since, being a Japanese institution, it needs yen income to meet yen expenses in the form of pensions, insurance claims and so forth.

The anomaly is that the Japanese government is forcing both borrowers and investors to raise or invest money outside Japan. It is possible for a

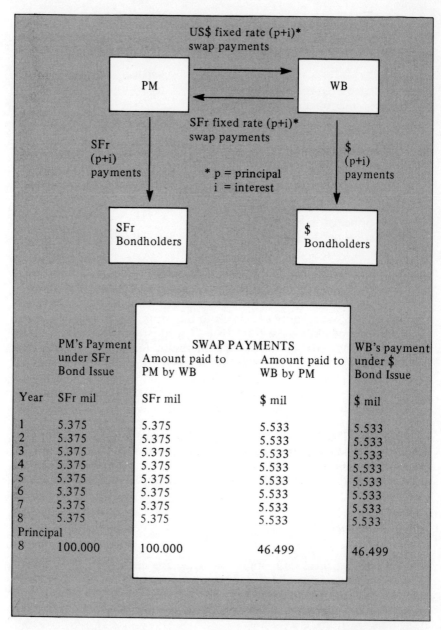

US$ fixed rate (p+i)*
swap payments

SFr fixed rate (p+i)*
swap payments

* p = principal
  i = interest

		SWAP PAYMENTS		
	PM's Payment under SFr Bond Issue	Amount paid to PM by WB	Amount paid to WB by PM	WB's payment under $ Bond Issue
Year	SFr mil	SFr mil	$ mil	$ mil
1	5.375	5.375	5.533	5.533
2	5.375	5.375	5.533	5.533
3	5.375	5.375	5.533	5.533
4	5.375	5.375	5.533	5.533
5	5.375	5.375	5.533	5.533
6	5.375	5.375	5.533	5.533
7	5.375	5.375	5.533	5.533
8	5.375	5.375	5.533	5.533
Principal				
8	100.000	100.000	46.499	46.499

currency swap to be arranged to swap the Japanese government borrower out of a dollar debt into yen debt, and the Japanese investor, in this example, out of dollar assets into a yen asset.

Because of Ministry of Finance regulations in Japan, it is not possible to match the Japanese government borrower directly with the Japanese investor, or for the Japanese investor to buy the Japanese government borrower's yankee bond issue. Any swap-linked securities transaction would require a foreign international bank ('FIB') with a branch in Japan, but head office outside Japan, to act as an intermediary, and for that bank or investment bank to locate a suitable borrower (non-Japanese) who can issue dollar bonds which meet the Japanese investor's credit requirements and can be bought by Japanese investors. Finding a suitable borrower is the key to making the transaction work.

The swap is in three parts: (1) The Japanese government borrower ('JGB') would enter into a swap with FIB's head office; (2) The Japanese investor ('JI') would enter into a swap with FIB's Japanese branch; and (3) FIB's Japanese branch and FIB's head office would then enter into a mirror swap.

Again the case study is based on a question and answer basis to illustrate the steps involved in working out respective costs in generating simulated fixed-rate finance through the swap.

Given information

1. JGB borrows dollars on the following terms:

amount	$100,000,000
interest rate (coupon)	$11\frac{1}{2}\%$ payable semi-annually
maturity	7 years
issue cost	$1\frac{3}{8}\%$
expenses	$400,000

2. JGB is prepared to swap out of its dollar debt into simulated yen obligation at a targeted all-in cost of yen 7.6% on an annual compounding basis.

3. JI is prepared to buy dollar denominated Eurobonds, but wishes to swap out of a dollar asset into a simulated yen asset, with a targeted return on assets of yen 8% on an annual compounding basis.

4. FIB requires a $\frac{1}{4}\%$ per annum fee for standing in the middle.

5. The current exchange rate is $1 = yen 240.

Questions

1. Determine the terms and conditions which need to attach to a dollar Eurobond issue to be sold to JI.

2. Construct a cash flow diagram showing the cash flows involved, and list the cash flows under JGB's bond issue, JI's Eurobond asset, and respective payments under the currency swap agreements.

Solution

Q. 1. Determine the terms and conditions which need to attach to a dollar Eurobond issue to be sold to JI

(Note: all figures are calculated on basis of $100,000,000 yankee bond issue, and expressed in millions.)

Step 1

Determine the net proceeds of the yankee bond issue by JGB:

issue price	$100.000
less: cost – commission	1.375
– expenses	.400
net proceeds	$ 98.225

Step 2

Convert the net proceeds in step 1 above to yen at the current exchange rate:

present value	$ 98.225
exchange rate	$1 = Y 240
nominal yen equivalent	Y23, 574.000

Step 3

Determine the amount of yen interest JGB will pay on the yen principal calculated in step 2 above to give JGB's targeted all-in cost of 7.6% annually:

yen principal	Y23,574.000
interest (all in cost 7.6%)	7.6%
interest	Y 1,791.624

Step 4

Determine the present value of yen payments JGB is prepared to make at JI's desired return on assets of 8% in yen annually:

number of years	=7	(n)
yield to maturity	=8%	(i)
interest (as per step 3 above)	=Y 1,791.62	(PMT)
principal (as per step 2 above)	=Y23,574.00	(FV)
present value	=Y23,083.06	(PV)

(Note: this is the amount JI will spend on buying dollar bonds.)

Step 5

Convert the present value of the yen principal above to dollars at current exchange rate:

present value yen principal	=Y23,083.06
exchange rate	$1 = Yen 240
present value dollar equivalent	=$96.179

Step 6

Calculate the required yield to maturity on dollar bonds to be purchased:

present value (as per step 5)	=96.179% (PV)
interest (paid semi-annually)	=11.5% (PMT)

(start)	1.011983 Enter	(See	$=1.011983$
(fin)	1.011990	Note)	$=1.011990$
F YTM			$=12.33\%$ (semi-annual compounding)
			$=12.71\%$ (annual compounding)

(Note: the above uses a programme for determining yields on US Treasury bonds. This assumes the Future Value (FV) to be 100%, 1.011983 is the assumed purchase date, ie, January 1, 1983 and 1.011990 is the assumed maturity date, ie, January 1, 1990, equivalent to a 7-year maturity (ie, $n=7$) and F YTM = yield to maturity. We use this programme because we are dealing with a yankee bond which pays interest semi-annually.)

Step 7

Adjust the payment in step 6 above, by 25 basis points, representing FIB's fees, and recalculate the yield to maturity:

PV	$=96.179$
PMT (paid semi-annually)	$=11.75\%$
(start) enter	$=1.011983$
(fin)	$=1.011990$
F YTM	$=12.58\%$ (semi-annual compounding)
	$=12.98\%$ (annual compounding)

Step 8

Determine the interest rate (coupon) on the proposed bond issue given the following information (ie, annual payment):

issue price (step 5)	$=96.179\%$	
costs	$=2.000\%$	
present value	$=94.179\%$	(PV)
years to maturity (step 7)	$=7$	(n)
future value	$=100\%$	(FV)
yield to maturity	$=12.98\%$ annual	(i)
interest (coupon)	$=11.66\%$ annual	(PMT)

Conclusion

To match the cash flows and meet all parties' objectives, FIB or another investment bank would have to find an issuer of acceptable credit rating to JI who would issue $100,000,000 of 7-year bonds at an issue price of 96.179%, with front-end (arrangement) costs of 2% and an interest rate (coupon) of 11.66% paid annually to give an all-in cost to the borrower of 12.98% on an annual compounding basis. (Note: this solution assumes that FIB is prepared to assume the mismatch on the dollar payments: paying dollars semi-annually to JGB but receiving dollars annually from JI.)

Summary of logic

In order to determine the terms of the dollar issue it is first necessary to convert the net proceeds of JGB's yankee bond issue to yen at the spot rate as JGB's target yen borrowing cost will determine the amount of yen it is willing to pay under the swap. This in turn determines the amount of yen available to be paid to JI under the swap. By discounting these yen payments at JI's desired return on assets ('ROA'), the calculation determines the amount of yen JI is prepared to sell spot for dollars to buy dollar Eurobonds. The income from these bonds will be used via the swap to service JGB dollar borrowing costs which is known from the given information. From the foregoing, the terms of a dollar bond issue can be determined in order to generate sufficient dollars to pay JGB via a swap.

Q. 2. Future payments

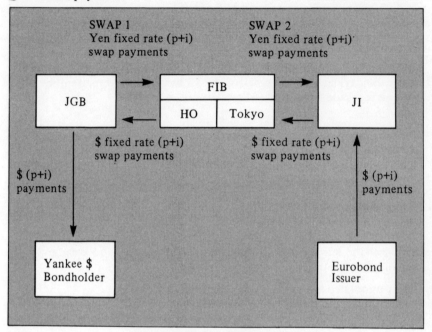

CASH FLOW SCHEDULE

Years	Payments by JGB to yankee bondholders	Swap 1		Swap 2		Receipts by JI from Eurobond Issuer
		Amount of $s paid by FIB to JGB	Amount of Yen paid by FIB to JGB	Amount of Yen paid by FIB to JI	Amount of $s paid by JI to FIB	
	$mm	$mm	Ybn	Ybn	$mm	$mm
Interest						
½	5.75	5.75				
1	5.75	5.75	1.792	1.792	11.66	11.66
1½	5.75	5.75				
2	5.75	5.75	1.792	1.792	11.66	11.66
2½	5.75	5.75				
3	5.75	5.75	1.792	1.792	11.66	11.66
3½	5.75	5.75				
4	5.75	5.75	1.792	1.792	11.66	11.66
4½	5.75	5.75				
5	5.75	5.75	1.792	1.792	11.66	11.66
5½	5.75	5.75				
6	5.75	5.75	1.792	1.792	11.66	11.66
6½	5.75	5.75				
7	5.75	5.75	1.792	1.792	11.66	11.66
Principal						
7	100.00	100.00	23.574	23.574	100.00	100.00

CROSS-CURRENCY FLOATING-TO-FIXED SWAP

A cross-currency fixed-to-floating debt swap combines the coupon swap with the fixed-to-fixed cross-currency swap in that one party converts fixed-rate finance in one currency to floating-rate finance in another, including principal payments at maturity.

The great popularity of interest rate swaps has resulted in fixed-rate bank paper becoming less desirable in the Eurobond market and credit spread differentials gradually being arbitraged away. Consequently, non-dollar based banks still face the question of how to fund their medium-term floating-rate dollar assets with medium-term floating-rate dollar liabilities. One solution would be for the various central banks to allow the banks under their jurisdictions to use their domestic fixed-rate borrowing strength in order to generate term floating-rate dollar finance by entering into cross-currency fixed-to-floating debt swap with suitable counterparties. For example, a German bank could raise fixed-rate Deutschemarks and swap into floating-rate dollars. A number of cross-currency fixed-to-floating debt swaps have already been arranged and the number is expected to increase, (although the Bundesbank has for the moment imposed restrictions on German banks using this technique).

The easiest way to describe this type of swap is by example. For instance, Company 'A' may borrow SFr 100 million for five years at 6% payable annually while Company 'B' may borrow the dollar equivalent of SFr 100 million, say, $50 million, for five years at LIBOR plus a margin (say, $\frac{1}{2}$%) payable semi-annually. Under a swap agreement between Company 'A' and Company 'B', Company 'A' would agree to pay to Company 'B' dollars equal to the interest payments and principal repayment due under Company 'B's' floating-rate loan on the appropriate future payment dates, in return for Company 'B' paying to Company 'A' Swiss francs equal to the interest payments and principal repayment due under Company 'A's' Swiss franc fixed-rate loan. Effectively, Company 'A' acts as a surrogate borrower of fixed-rate Swiss francs for Company 'B' and Company 'B' as a surrogate borrower of floating-rate dollars for Company 'A'. This transaction can be depicted as shown on p. 52.

Case study: 1

The first known swap transaction of this type was arranged in July 1981. It is worthwhile considering this transaction as it was an interesting variation on the above-mentioned example. The transaction was between the French car company, Renault (which required fixed-rate yen finance), and one of the major Japanese security houses, Yamaichi (which was acting as principal for a number of Japanese institutional investors). It involved Yamaichi purchasing US dollar denominated floating-rate notes and Renault raising (or utilising existing) floating-rate dollar debt. As a result of the transaction, Renault was able through its ability to borrow floating-rate dollar finance to simulate a fixed-rate yen borrowing at a time when it was unable for regulatory reasons to borrow fixed-rate yen finance.

Japanese investors were able to buy foreign assets, an action being encouraged by the Japanese Ministry of Finance, which also diversified their portfolio, and at the same time hedge their dollar investment back into yen. The yield they received was also higher than that available on other yen fixed-rate investments. This transaction can be depicted as follows.

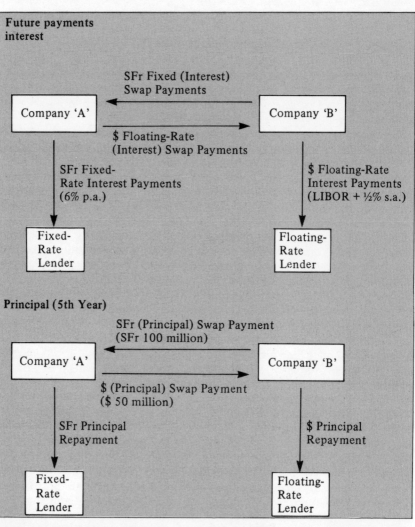

Future payments interest

SFr Fixed (Interest) Swap Payments

Company 'A' ← Company 'B'

$ Floating-Rate (Interest) Swap Payments →

SFr Fixed-Rate Interest Payments (6% p.a.)

$ Floating-Rate Interest Payments (LIBOR + ½% s.a.)

Fixed-Rate Lender

Floating-Rate Lender

Principal (5th Year)

SFr (Principal) Swap Payment (SFr 100 million)

Company 'A' ← Company 'B'

$ (Principal) Swap Payment ($ 50 million) →

SFr Principal Repayment

$ Principal Repayment

Fixed-Rate Lender

Floating-Rate Lender

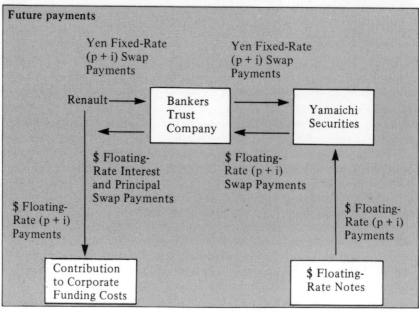

Future payments

Yen Fixed-Rate (p + i) Swap Payments

Yen Fixed-Rate (p + i) Swap Payments

Renault → Bankers Trust Company → Yamaichi Securities

$ Floating-Rate Interest and Principal Swap Payments

$ Floating-Rate (p + i) Swap Payments

$ Floating-Rate (p + i) Payments

$ Floating-Rate (p + i) Payments

Contribution to Corporate Funding Costs

$ Floating-Rate Notes

Case study: 2

To consider the cross currency fixed-to-floating debt swap in depth and to illustrate a different application, the following case study analyzes another actual transaction involving the first known pre-syndicated joint swap and loan. It involves a financing for Azienda Autonoma delle Ferrovie dello Stato ('Ferrovie'), the Italian State Railway, arranged jointly by Bankers Trust International Limited ('BTI') and Soditic SA. The Appendix to this Chapter (p 61, post) sets out a 'tombstone' showing the banks involved.

Structure

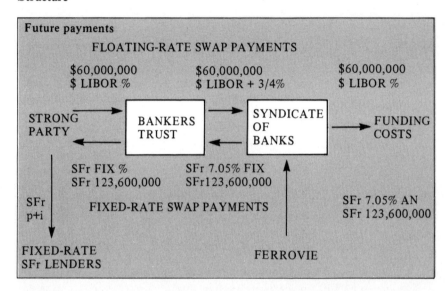

Soditic successfully received a mandate from Ferrovie to lead manage a syndicated fixed-rate Swiss franc loan. Final terms of this loan were as follows:

Amount:	SFr 211,600,000
Interest:	7.05% payable annually
Redemption:	in one lump sum at maturity
Maturity:	April 28, 1988

Certain of the participating banks participated in a syndicated swap under which they sold their future Swiss franc receipts, equivalent to 7.05% payable annually based on a principal amount of SFr 123,600,000 each year, for the next five years and a principal amount at the end of the fifth year of SFr 123,600,000 to Bankers Trust Company ('BTCo') in return for BTCo selling to the banks every six months for the next five years interest equivalent to six-month LIBOR plus ¾% based on a principal amount of $60,000,000 and a principal amount at the end of the fifth year of $60,000,000.

Conversely BTI received two mandates from strong parties who wished effectively to convert fixed-rate Swiss franc liabilities into simulated floating-rate liabilities. Under this agreement the strong parties agreed to pay dollar interest to BTCo on a (LIBOR priced) floating-rate basis and a dollar principal amount at the end of the fifth year. In return BTCo agreed to sell Swiss franc interest to the strong parties on a fixed-rate basis and a Swiss franc principal amount at the end of the fifth year.

Objectives (or why)

Strong parties:	wanted to raise attractively priced floating rate-dollar finance.
Syndicate of banks:	interested in lending to Ferrovie but unable or unwilling to fund themselves in Swiss francs.
Ferrovie:	wanted to borrow fixed-rate Swiss francs but in an amount greater than the Swiss capital market would stand.

Results

Strong parties:	Used their ability to raise fixed-rate Swiss francs and through their agreement with BTCo effectively transformed fixed-rate Swiss franc liabilities into floating-rate dollar liabilities.
Syndicate of banks:	Transformed a Swiss franc fixed-rate asset into a simulated floating-rate dollar asset which allowed the banks to fund themselves on a floating-rate dollar basis which eliminated their problem of being unable or unwilling to fund themselves on a fixed-rate Swiss franc basis.
Ferrovie:	Successfully raised fixed-rate Swiss francs in an amount and for a maturity which otherwise (ie, without the swap) they may not have been able to raise.

The crux of this transaction can be summarised as follows:

The strong parties via the swap mechanism indirectly acted as a surrogate borrower of fixed-rate Swiss francs for Ferrovie who in turn, and indirectly via the syndicated bank swap, acted as a surrogate borrower of floating-rate dollars.

Details of the offer telex sent to the participating banks are set out in the Appendix to this Chapter (p. 61).

SAME CURRENCY FLOATING-TO-FLOATING SWAPS

The last major form of swap is the floating-to-floating debt swap. In terms of concept and difficulty, it is the simplest form. To date the most popular form of floating-to-floating swap has been the Prime/LIBOR swap. This swap involves an agreement between two parties whereby one party agrees to sell an amount calculated by reference to a floating interest rate such as LIBOR to another party, in return for the other party selling to the first party an amount of interest calculated on a pre-determined basis such as US prime. Both calculations are based on the same notional principal amount with rate settings determined by reference banks and payment dates agreed in advance.

According to market sources, the first prime/LIBOR swap arose out of a rescheduling of debt for certain Latin American countries. A large portion of this debt was repriced on a prime rate basis. This suited the American banks, for whom prime pricing did not represent a funding risk and was more favourable than LIBOR. For the non-dollar based banks, however, there was a substantial funding risk as they had no means of generating prime priced liabilities to fund these repriced assets. The US banks had substantial LIBOR-priced assets which they could fund more profitably on a prime basis while the European banks would prefer to have LIBOR-priced assets as opposed to prime-priced assets. Out of these diverse needs arose the opportunity for the US Banks to swap with the non-dollar banks or European banks.

Under such an arrangement, the European banks sold the income on their prime-priced assets to the US banks in return for the US banks selling the income on their LIBOR-priced assets to the European banks.

Case study

Again, according to market sources, one of the more recent loan syndications involving a prime/LIBOR swap was a syndicated loan to Ireland. A US bank formed a syndicate of international banks which were offered participations in both a prime-priced and/or a LIBOR-priced loan. It is understood that as a separate transaction, which did not involve the Government of Ireland, the European banks were offered the ability to subscribe for the prime portion of the loan together with a swap, under which they would sell their prime-priced income stream for a LIBOR-priced income stream, the result of which would give them a more attractive return than if they subscribed for the LIBOR-priced portion of the loan directly.

It is fundamental to note that the only point that links the swap and the loan is that they both have common rate setting times and payment dates (and most probably common rate setting banks). If we consider the terms and conditions for the syndicated loan and the (assumed) terms and conditions of the swap from the European banks' point of view, this importance can be easily demonstrated:

Loan	*Prime*	*LIBOR*
Borrower	Ireland	Ireland
Amount		$500,000,000
Interest	The higher of Prime or 90-day CD's plus 1/4%	6-month LIBOR plus $\frac{1}{2}$% for years 1 to 3, and 5/8% for years 4 to 7
Payment dates	Quarterly in arrears	Semi-annually in arrears
Redemption	7 years	7 years
Final maturity	4 years grace plus 7 equal semi-annual instalments of principal	
Swap		
Notional principal amount	$100,000,000	$100,000,000

(Note: notional principal amount amortises in line with amortisation of loan.)

Swap payments:

Interest receipt
— Amount to be paid   6-month LIBOR plus
  by US bank to   5/8 for years 1 to 3, and
  European bank   3/4% for years 4 to 7

Interest payments
— Amount to be paid   The higher of prime
  by European bank to   or 90-day CD's plus
  US bank   1/4%

Payment dates:
  US bank to European   Semi-annually in arrears
  bank
  European bank to US   Quarterly in arrears
  bank

Maturity: 7 years   7 years

(Note: CD = Negotiable dollar certificates of deposit.)

First however, the swap should be diagramatically represented and the cash flows listed from the European bank's point of view as follows.

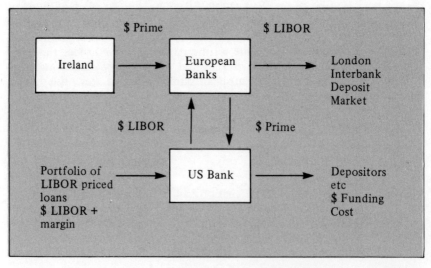

Cash flows under the swap from the European banks' point of view are:

Payment date	Receipts under syndicated loan	Swap — Amounts paid to USB by EB	Swap — Amounts received by EB from USB	Net cash flow
Quarter				
1	$P \times$ (Pr or CD) $+\frac{1}{4}\%$	$NP \times$ (Pr or CD) $+\frac{1}{4}\%$		
2	,,	,,	$L+\frac{5}{8}\%$	$L+5\frac{5}{8}\%$
3 to 12	The above cash flows are repeated up to the end of the 12th quarter (or 3rd year)			

Payment date	Receipts under syndicated loan	Swap		Net cash flow
		Amounts paid to USB by EB	Amounts received by EB from USB	
13 to 28	The following cash flows are repeated from 13th quarter to maturity			
13	$P \times (Pr \text{ or } CD) + \frac{1}{4}\%$	$NP \times (Pr \text{ or } CD) + \frac{1}{4}\%$	$\left. \begin{array}{c} \\ \\ \end{array} \right\}$	
14	,,	,,	$L + \frac{3}{4}\%$	$L + \frac{3}{4}\%$

Note: P = Principal/NP = Notional Principal
       PR = Prime
       CD = Negotiable Certificate of Deposit (90-day)
       L = London Interbank Offered Rate – LIBOR (6-month)

By examining the European banks' cash flows, it can be seen that, by coupling a swap with a syndicated loan, the European banks have effectively transformed a prime-priced asset into a simulated LIBOR-priced asset. If there are to be no cash implications for the European banks, the cash payments made under the swap have to be made on the same day to the US banks as the interest due from Ireland is received; hence the need for common payments. Also, for the actual amounts received and paid to be the same, the rate determination, down to the last decimal point, under the loan and swap agreements have to be the same.

Other types

Apart from prime/LIBOR swaps, other floating-to-floating swaps are gaining in popularity among banks, such as prime/91 day treasury bill swaps and LIBOR/91 day treasury bill swaps. As with all swaps, there must be a reason, a logic or an anomaly for them to work. Usually the logic transforms into cost savings or a reduction of risk. The following graph illustrates hypothetically the risks a bank faces when the nature of the income from its assets differs from the interest expense on its liabilities.

The graph is based on the following example.

A bank, B, invests in a six-month LIBOR asset, with the interest rate initially set at 10% for the first six months, as shown by the **red line.**

B funds this asset by borrowing day-to-day funds at initially 9%, the day-to-day cost of these funds being represented by the black line. At the end of the second month, the cost of these funds rises steeply to approximately 11.5% and remains around that level for several months to come. The broken line plots the day-to-day six-month work rate over the period concerned. By comparing the broken line (day-to-day cost of six-month LIBOR) against the black line (day-to-day cost of funds) it can be seen that day-to-day six-month LIBOR exceeds day-to-day cost of funds. From B's point of view however, it has a six-month asset-yielding 10% and the pricing/yield on this asset is not adjusted until the end of the six months. Meanwhile its cost of funds has risen from approximately 9% to $11\frac{1}{2}\%$, putting it in a loss situation. The striped area represents B's profit while the dotted area represents B's loss. This funding risk illustrated by the graph, on p. 58, is an important reason why floating-to-floating swaps should flourish in the future. If B were to write a LIBOR/average LIBOR swap under which, eg, it would receive six-month LIBOR weekly reset paid semi-annually in return for paying six-month LIBOR semi-annually, it would reduce this funding risk.

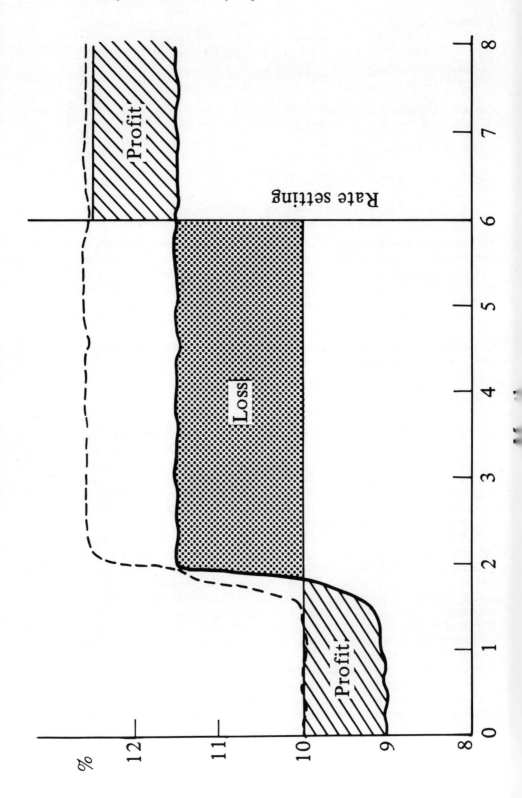

CROSS-CURRENCY FLOATING-TO-FLOATING SWAPS

The final, though least important, form of swaps is the cross-currency floating-to-floating swap. This type of swap has not been fully developed since the same result can often be achieved through the forward foreign exchange market, which is characterised by liquidity efficiency and convenience. Consequently, cross-currency floating-to-floating swaps are unlikely to serve as a viable alternative to the foreign exchange market. However, there are situations in which this form of swap is useful. For example, to sell forward Swiss francs for dollars for six months is normal, but to have a term commitment which would roll over this contract every six months for the next five years is not market practice, and currently not feasible. A swap could achieve this.

A cross-currency floating-to-floating swap can be simply defined as an agreement between two parties under which one party agrees to pay an amount equal to the principal and interest payments under, eg, the other party's Swiss franc floating rate debt, in return for the other party paying an amount equal to the principal and interest payments due under, eg, the first party's floating rate dollar debt.

Example

Assume Swiss party borrows SFr 250,000,000 on a floating rate basis at 6-month LIBOR for five years, while a US party borrows $100,000,000 on a floating rate basis at six-month LIBOR. Both parties enter into a floating-to-floating cross currency debt swap. The swap can be diagrammatically represented as follows.

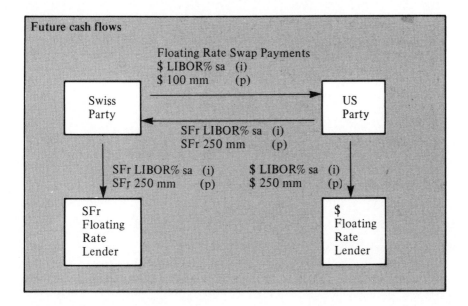

The cash flows under such a swap transaction in respect of the Swiss party are as follows:

Swap Receipts/Payments

Period	Payments to SFr lenders	Payments to US Party	Receipts from US party	Net cash flow
$\frac{1}{2}$	SFr LIBOR %	$ LIBOR %	SFr LIBOR %	$ LIBOR %
1	,,	,,	,,	,,
$1\frac{1}{2}$	,,	,,	,,	,,
2	,,	,,	,,	,,
$2\frac{1}{2}$	,,	,,	,,	,,
3	,,	,,	,,	,,
$3\frac{1}{2}$	,,	,,	,,	,,
4	,,	,,	,,	,,
$4\frac{1}{2}$	,,	,,	,,	,,
5	,,	,,	,,	,,
5	SFr 250 mm	$ 100 mm	SFr 250 mm	$ 100 mm

As a result of the above transaction, the Swiss party converts a floating-rate Swiss franc liability into a simulated floating-rate dollar liability, while the US party converts a floating-rate dollar liability into a simulated floating-rate Swiss franc liability.

Appendix

June 1983

CURRENCY EXCHANGE AGREEMENT

US$ 60,000,000 / Swiss Francs 123,600,000

Principals:

BANKERS TRUST COMPANY

and:

BANCO EXTERIOR (SUIZA) S.A.	BANQUE INDOSUEZ
CIBC FINANZ AG	LLOYDS BANK INTERNATIONAL LTD.
LTCB (SCHWEIZ) AG	MITSUBISHI FINANZ (SCHWEIZ) AG
BANCO DI NAPOLI INTERNATIONAL S.A.	BANCO DI SICILIA
BANK OF MONTREAL	THE BANK OF NOVA SCOTIA CHANNEL
INTERNATIONAL COMMERCIAL BANK plc	ISLANDS LTD.
PRIVATBANKEN LIMITED	ISTITUTO BANCARIO SAN PAOLO DI TORINO
BANCO DI SANTO SPIRITO	THE INDUSTRIAL BANK OF KUWAIT KSC
(LUXEMBOURG) S.A.	BANQUE EUROPÉENNE DE TOKYO S.A.
FIRST INTERSTATE BANK OF CALIFORNIA	CHRISTIANIA BANK LUXEMBOURG S.A.

Arranged jointly by

BANKERS TRUST INTERNATIONAL LIMITED

and

SODITIC S.A.

Agent:

LLOYDS BANK INTERNATIONAL LTD.

The above transaction forms part of a funding arrangement on behalf of the above mentioned banks in relation to the following loan

Azienda Autonoma delle Ferrovie dello Stato

Swiss Francs 211,600,000 Fixed Rate Loan Due 1988

Lead Manager:

SODITIC S.A.

Funds provided by

American Express Bank (Switzerland) AG	Banco Exterior (Suiza) S.A.
Banco di Santo Spirito (Luxembourg) S.A.	Banco di Napoli International S.A.
Banco di Sicilia – London Branch	Bank in Liechtenstein AG
Bank of Montreal	The Bank of Nova Scotia Channel Islands Ltd.
Bankers Trust AG	Bankers Trust GmbH
Banque Bruxelles Lambert (Suisse) S.A.	Banque Européenne de Tokyo S.A.
Banque Indosuez	Banque Indosuez, Succursales de Suisse
Banque Louis-Dreyfus en Suisse S.A.	Banque de Paris et des Pays-Bas (Suisse) S.A.
Banque de l'Union Européenne	Banque de l'Union Européenne en Suisse S.A.
Chemical Bank	Christiania Bank Luxembourg S.A.
CIBC Finanz AG	Compagnie de Banque et de Crédit S.A.
Dow Banking Corporation	First Interstate Limited
The Industrial Bank of Kuwait KSC	International Commercial Bank plc
Istituto Bancario San Paolo di Torino – London Branch –	Lavoro Bank AG
Lloyds Bank International Ltd.	LTCB (Schweiz) AG
Mitsubishi Finanz (Schweiz) AG	Nederlandsche Middenstandsbank (Suisse) S.A.
Privatbanken Limited	Privat Kredit Bank
Soditic S.A.	United Overseas Bank
Zürcher Kantonalbank	

Agent:

Lloyds Bank International Ltd.

OFFERING TELEX

RE: Syndicated loan of up to SFr 200,000,000 for Azienda
Autonoma delle Ferrovie dello Stato, Rome, Italy

To be optionally funded through a floating-rate dollar/fixed-rate Swiss franc swap with Bankers Trust Company.

We are pleased to invite you to join the above mentioned syndicated loan on the following terms and conditions.

Borrower:	Azienda Autonoma delle Ferrovie dello Stato, Rome, Italy (FS).
Security:	By virtue of Italian law, this loan will represent direct and unconditional obligations of the Republic of Italy.
Amount:	Up to SFr 200,000,000 (equivalent to US Dollars 100 million).
Purpose:	The net proceeds of this loan will serve for the partial financing of the investment programme of FS according to law no. 17 of February 12, 1982.
Final maturity:	5 years from date of drawdown.
Repayment:	In one bullet repayment 5 years from date of drawdown.
Prepayment:	None.
Interest:	7.05 per cent p.a., payable annually in arrears and to be calculated for 30 days a month and 360 days a year.
Drawdown:	In one tranche within one month from date of signing, exact date to be advised later.
Documentation:	The loan will be evidenced by a standard Euroloan agreement among the borrower, the manager and the lending banks. It will contain clauses standard for this type of transaction: There will be an optional separate currency and interest swap agreement ('swap') which will convert each lending bank's 6-month floating-rate LIBOR-based dollar funding into fixed rate Swiss francs. This will permit each lending bank to match fund its fixed-rate loan. The swap agreement will be between Bankers Trust Company and the lending banks, severally, and will be subject to New York law.
Taxation:	All payments under the loan shall be made free and clear of any present or future withholding taxes or other similar charges of whatever nature in Italy.
Governing law:	Loan agreement: the law of Switzerland Swap agreement: New York law
Authorisations:	All authorisations required in Italy and in Switzerland are to be issued in the name of Soditic SA, Geneva. This loan is subject to obtaining authorisations from the Swiss National Bank and the Officio Italiano Dei Cambi.
Funding of the above loan	Although this is a fixed-rate Swiss franc loan, syndicate members will have the option to fund their participations through the floating-rate London Interbank Eurodollar Market. The option principal amount of each lending bank's Swiss franc participation (the 'dollar principal amount') will be determined by Bankers Trust Company using its Dollar/Swiss franc mid-rate. Each lending bank will deliver its dollar principal amount to the agent on the date of the loan and the agent will

deliver the dollar principal amount to Bankers Trust
Company against payment by Bankers Trust Company
of the Swiss franc amount of such lending bank's loan.
The Swiss franc amount will then be disbursed to the
borrower by the agent on behalf of the lending bank.
Every 6 months Bankers Trust Company will pay a
dollar amount equal to the interest on the dollar
principal amount, (calculated in the basis of the exact
number of days elapsed at 6 months LIBOR $+\frac{3}{4}$ percent
per annum) to the agent, who will distribute this amount
to the lending bank. Every 12 months, each lending
bank, through the agent, will pay to Bankers Trust
Company an amount in Swiss francs, equal to the
interest on such lending bank's Swiss franc loan,
(calculated at a rate of 7.05 percent per annum on the
Swiss franc amount of such lending bank's loan
calculated for 30 days a month and 360 days a year).
At final maturity each lending bank will pay to Bankers
Trust Company the principal amount of its Swiss franc
loan and in turn, Bankers Trust Company shall pay to
the agent for the account of the lending bank such bank's
dollar principal amount.

FS shall pay at the relevant maturities interest and
principal on its loan to the agent in Swiss francs, for
account of the lending banks, whose undertakings
towards Bankers Trust Company are independent from
receipt of such payments.

This transaction results in each lending bank exercising
the option having a Swiss franc loan to FS and a Swiss
franc contingent liability to Bankers Trust Company. At
the same time it results in the lending bank having a
dollar contingent asset from Bankers Trust Company
which will cover a dollar liability arising out of a dollar
LIBOR funding.

CHAPTER 5

Putting theory into practice

The major forms of swaps have now been covered and examples of how the product can be applied given. By now it should be apparent that the most important factor in understanding swap techniques is the recognition that they involve the buying and selling of cash flows, either fixed or variable, in the same or different currencies. By using Discounted Cash Flow (DCF) theory, the value of one cash flow can be compared with another. It should also be clear that an understanding of yield and DCF calculations is essential for comprehending and applying swap concepts.

Being able to put theory into practice is the ultimate test of whether one understands the principles. The following is a hypothetical case study based on an actual situation, illustrating how swap techniques can be used by a merchant bank in constructing financial packages to meet a client's needs.

Background

A French contractor (FC) successfully tendered for a large construction contract from a foreign government (FG). The contract qualified for export credit and insurance from the French export credit agency, COFACE. The contract price was denominated in Swiss francs. The majority of the goods and services due under the contract were manufactured or performed in France.

Although FC was content to tender in Swiss francs, FC was also interested in eliminating the foreign exchange exposure under the contract and in taking advantage of the interest differential prevailing between Swiss francs and French francs. The following table sets out FC's forecast cash flows under the contract:

Month	Sfr million	Month	Sfr million	Month	Sfr million
22	5.1	35	5.7	42	5.7
24	5.7	36	5.7	43	5.7
26	5.7	37	5.7	44	5.7
28	5.7	38	5.7	45	5.7
30	5.7	39	5.7	47	17.0
32	5.7	40	5.7	53	17.0
34	5.7	41	5.7	58	22.0

Problem

Given that FC was interested in locking-in the interest differential and eliminating currency exposure, how could a merchant bank analyse the situation and construct a package which would meet its client's requirements?

Assumption

It is possible to raise fixed-rate Swiss francs, but it is not possible to launch a fixed-rate French franc issue. A forward foreign exchange market exists in French francs and Swiss francs, but it is limited in size, subject to restrictive exchange controls and does not go beyond six to twelve months. A bank intermediary is available to act as principal for any swaps written between the two counterparties. The swap payments are designed in the form of an annuity.

Alternatives

A Merchant bank could try to find a counterparty with a matching French franc cash flow which would prefer to convert this cash flow into Swiss francs.
Comment
Given the varied nature of the cash flow and the maturities, it would be very difficult to find a counterparty to match FC.

B Merchant bank could search for a counterparty with a net asset exposure in French francs which would like to hedge its exposure.
Comment
A distinct possibility, but it may be difficult given the uneven nature and maturity of cash flow. It could appeal to a parent wishing to hedge future dividend payments from its French subsidiary. Alternatively, a swap could be written with a number of parties for either hedging net worth or dividend remittances.

C Merchant bank could find an entity which wanted to borrow French francs or create a French franc liability, was unable to do so because of Government regulations and unfavourable market conditions in the French franc capital market, and at the same time is of sufficient quality or credit standing to borrow in other capital markets.
Comment
Given restrictive controls in France, lack of a domestic fixed-rate market, expected and continued devaluation of the French franc, fixed-rate French franc liabilities are a scarce item.

Of the above alternatives, C would appear to have the highest probability of success. For example, an agency like Electricite de France (EDF), an AAA rated agency (assuming Ministry of Finance approval) with high capital expenditure commitments, would be a logical counterparty. Another consideration is the size of the transaction. Logically, a capital markets transaction plus a swap is virtually the only practical solution to meeting FC's requirements.

Solution

Persuade EDF to borrow fixed-rate Swiss francs and enter into a cross-currency fixed-to-fixed debt/asset swap, via a bank principal (BP), under which EDF would transform a fixed-rate Swiss franc liability into a simulated fixed-rate French franc liability and FC would in turn transform a deferred Swiss franc asset into a deferred simulated French franc asset.

Having determined the optimal way of meeting FC's needs, the next step is to design a capital markets transaction: a Swiss franc issue which would create the cash flow necessary to meet FC's requirements but still conform with Swiss capital market convention. It should be noted that, in practice, it would be impossible to create an issue which would fit perfectly. However, using a bank intermediary which can manage long or short Swiss franc positions, this problem can be overcome. Also, it is possible under a bank private placement to have a more flexible repayment schedule.

Designing the package: EDF

The following sets out a suggested method for working out the terms of a Swiss franc issue by EDF, the terms and conditions for a cross-currency fixed-to-fixed debt swap between EDF and BP, and a cross-currency fixed-to-fixed asset swap between FC and BP, such that all parties' objectives are satisfied. It is not an optimal solution, as no account has been taken of interest earned on surplus balances nor techniques such as reducing or increasing the average life of the various simulated currency liabilities and assets utilised.

The essential tool for designing a package is to set up a cash flow spread sheet as shown in the Appendix to this chapter (p. 71).

1. Determine, by trial and error basis, the maximum size of a Swiss franc private placement to be undertaken by EDF, given the following constraints, market information and given information:
   (a) FC Swiss franc cash flows known (See Schedule A of the Appendix to this Chapter);
   (b) all-in cost for EDF raising three-year Swiss francs is approximately 6.50% (annual compound (PV = 98, n = 3, Pymt = 5.75%, FV = 100));
   (c) EDF requires a minimum average life of three years;
   (d) EDF will not pay more than $14\frac{1}{2}\%$ on an all-in cost basis (annual compounding) for generating simulated French franc liabilities;
   (e) under Swiss National Bank regulations, it is assumed that no principal repayment is permitted within the first two years, and that the average life must be greater than half the final maturity.
   In order to determine the size of EDF's Swiss franc private placement, the first step is to discount FC's future Swiss franc cash flow at EDF's Swiss franc all-in cost borrowing rate of 6.5% to determine the present value. This amounts to SFr 127.14 million. By a trial and error basis, and by reference to FC's future Swiss franc cash flows which effectively service this debt, we can then establish that EDF could issue a private placement of SFr 140,000,000 at $5\frac{3}{4}\%$ with a final maturity of five years. The following sets out the cash flow schedule under the private placement.

Years	Principal	Interest	Principal repayment	Total payment	New principal	% of original principal
			Figures in millions			
$\frac{1}{2}$	140.00	4.03	0.00	4.03	140.00	100.00
1	140.00	4.02	0.00	4.02	140.00	100.00
$1\frac{1}{2}$	140.00	4.03	0.00	4.03	140.00	100.00
2	140.00	4.02	6.78	10.80	133.22	100.00

$2\frac{1}{2}$	133.22	3.83	13.27	17.10	119.95	95.16
3	119.95	3.45	19.35	22.80	100.60	85.69
$3\frac{1}{2}$	100.60	2.89	31.31	34.20	69.29	71.86
4	69.29	1.99	32.11	34.10	37.18	49.49
$4\frac{1}{2}$	37.18	1.07	15.93	17.00	21.25	26.56
5	21.25	0.61	21.25	21.86	0.00	15.18

The trial and error basis involved juggling with the size of the issue, the principal repayment and the amount of Swiss francs in BP's hand as per Schedule F in the Appendix to this chapter.

By adding the percentage outstanding of principal for each year, and dividing by 200, the average life can be determined: 3.72 years.

2. Determine the principal amount of the simulated French franc borrowing by converting the net proceeds of the Swiss franc private placement to French francs at the prevailing spot Swiss franc/French franc exchange rate of SFr 1 = FFr 3.80:

	SFr	FFr
	(in millions)	
Swiss franc private placement	140.00	
Issue cost (2%)	2.80	
Swap arrangement fee*	0.36	
Swiss franc net proceeds	136.84	
French franc equivalent @ SFr 1 = FFr 3.80		520.00

3. Determine a principal and interest payment schedule (on an annuity basis), given that there are no Swiss franc interest rate receipts under the swap until the twenty-second month to service EDF's Swiss franc debt. This problem is overcome by assuming no principal repayments, only interest in the first two periods and then retiring the debt by seven equal semi-annual annuity payments. It was also decided to shorten the final maturity from five years to four and a half years.

The amount of the annuity payment is determined by solving for the payment (PMT) amount which is calculated to be 96.50 given the following information:

number of periods	(n)	7
present value	(Pv)	520
yield to maturity	(i)	7.0047%
future value	(Fv)	0

There are no set rules for determining repayments, bearing in mind whatever is designed has to be logical, practical and suit the client and the market.

The other important factor is that EDF will not pay more than $14\frac{1}{2}\%$, on an all-in cost basis compounding. This is equivalent to a yield of 14.01% on a semi-annual compounding basis.

The following sets out the cash flow schedule under EDF's simulated French franc liabilities.

---

* Swap arrangement fee in this case is a rounding item.

Years	Principal	Interest	Principal repayment	Total (annuity) payment	New principal	% of original principal
				(French franc millions)		
$\frac{1}{2}$	520.00	36.42		36.42	520.00	100.00
1	520.00	36.42		36.42	520.00	100.00
$1\frac{1}{2}$	520.00	36.42	60.08	96.50	459.92	100.00
2	459.92	32.21	64.29	96.50	395.63	88.45
$2\frac{1}{2}$	395.63	27.71	68.79	96.50	326.84	76.08
3	326.64	22.89	73.61	96.50	253.23	62.85
$3\frac{1}{2}$	253.23	17.74	78.76	96.50	174.47	48.70
4	174.47	12.22	84.28	96.50	90.19	33.56
$4\frac{1}{2}$	90.19	6.31	90.19	96.50	0.00	17.34

The all-in cost of the above loan can be calculated by finding the discount figure which, when applied to the total repayment column, discounts them to give a PV of 520. The rate is 7.0047% semi-annually or on an annual compounding basis 14.50%.

4. One of EDF's requirements was that the average life of the simulated liability should exceed three years. Again, the average life is determined by adding up the percentage outstanding of principal for each year and dividing by 200, which gives 3.13 years.

We have now determined the following:

— terms of EDF's Swiss franc private placement and the resulting cash flows;
— EDF's cash flows under its simulated French franc liability.

Consequently, we are now in a position to write a swap between EDF and BP under which BP would sell Swiss francs to EDF to meet its payments due under its Swiss franc private placement, in return for EDF selling French francs to BP which it will, under a second swap, sell to FC in return for FC selling Swiss francs to BP.

Under the swap between EDF and BP, they would agree to buy and sell currencies as follows:

Value date (Yr)	EDF sells FFr to BP	BP sells SFr to EDF
	(in millions)	
$\frac{1}{2}$	36.42	4.03
1	36.42	4.02
$1\frac{1}{2}$	96.50	4.03
2	96.50	10.80
$2\frac{1}{2}$	96.50	17.10
3	96.50	22.80
$3\frac{1}{2}$	96.50	34.20
4	96.50	34.10
$4\frac{1}{2}$	96.50	17.00
5	0.00	21.86

Designing the package: FC

The next step is to determine the terms and conditions of the swap between FC and BP, the cash flows involved and cost benefits to FC.

1. To determine the cash flows under the swap, it is important to note that FC does not receive any Swiss francs under its contract until the twenty-second month, but BP has to make Swiss franc payments to cover payments to EDF. On the other hand, BP is long of French francs. Consequently, it goes into the forward foreign exchange market and sells French francs forward for Swiss francs, as follows.

Yr	BP's SFr Payments	BP's FFr Receipts	FFr Sold Forward	BP's FFr Balance	SFr Brought Forward	BP's SFr Balance
			In millions			
$\frac{1}{2}$	4.03	36.42	36.42	0.00	9.20	5.17
1	4.02	36.42	11.84	24.58	2.88	4.03
$1\frac{1}{2}$	4.03	96.50	N/A	N/A	N/A	N/A

Assumed forward rates: 6 months SFr 1 = FFr 3.96
    1 year   SFr 1 = FFr 4.11

So at the end of 6 months BP sells FFr 36.42 for SFr 9.20 and pays away SF 4.03 to EDF under the swap leaving BP with a SFr balance of SFr 5.17. At the end of 1 year BP again sell's French francs for Swiss francs and again pays EDF such that at the end of year one, BP has surplus Swiss francs of SFr 4.03, sufficient to meet the third period (year $1\frac{1}{2}$) Swiss franc interest payment. It is also long of FFr 24.58, which it can sell to FC.

2. We are now in a position to work out the amount of French francs available for sale by BP to FC. The amount available is FFr 24.58 at the end of period two, plus seven equal semi-annual instalments of FFr 96.50. In return, FC can sell its SFr cash flow, as previously listed, to BP.

   In order to determine the effective interest differential which can be locked in for FC, the PV of the future Swiss franc income stream has to be calculated, using a discount factor of 5.75% (ie, the coupon rate on EDF's SFr private placement). This comes to SFr 130.23 million which when converted to French francs at the spot rate of SFr 1 = FFr 3.80, gives a PV in French franc terms of FFr 494.87 Million.

   It is now possible to calculate FC's return in French francs, based on the French francs BP has available to pay FC as follows.

Yr	Principal	Interest @ 6.2453%	Capital Repayment	Total (annuity) payment	New principal	% of original principal
	In millions					
$\frac{1}{2}$	494.87	(30.91)	—	—	525.78	100.00
1	525.78	(32.83)	—	24.58	534.03	106.25
$1\frac{1}{2}$	534.03	33.35	63.15	96.50	470.88	107.91
2	470.88	29.41	67.09	96.50	403.79	95.15
$2\frac{1}{2}$	403.79	25.22	71.28	96.50	332.51	81.60
3	332.51	20.76	75.74	96.50	256.77	67.19
$3\frac{1}{2}$	256.77	16.04	80.46	96.50	176.31	51.89
4	176.31	11.01	85.49	96.50	90.82	35.63
$4\frac{1}{2}$	90.82	5.68	90.82	96.50	0.00	18.35

This calculation involves an iterative process, as interest during periods one and two has to be capitalised less the payment of FFr 24,580,000, to give a new principal amount at the end of period two of FFr 534,030,000. The yield or discount factor on an annuity of FFr 96,500,000 for seven years to give a PV of FFr 534,030,000 can then be calculated. The iterative process is involved as the interest rate used for calculating interest which is capitalised at the end of periods one and two to give a new principal amount has to be the same as the discount rate on the annuity. This yield is calculated to be 6.2453% per period, or on an annual compounding basis 12.88%.

A simpler way to do this calculation is to find the discount rate which, when applied to the total payment column above, discounts these amounts to give a PV of FFr 494,870,000.

Conclusion

Based on the above calculations, it is possible to lock in a yield differential of 7.13%, being the difference between the rate used to discount FC's Swiss franc cash flow of 5.75% and the above calculated French franc yield of 12.88%.

The overall transaction can be depicted as follows.

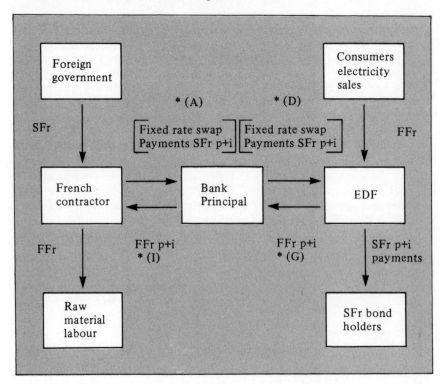

* Refers to column on cash flow schedule set out in Appendix 1, p 71, post.

FUTURE CASH FLOW SCHEDULE

CASH FLOW SPREAD SHEET (All figures in millions)

Month	FC Pays BP SFr A	BP pays EDF SFr i B	P C	Total D	BP Proceeds of Fwd Sale of FFr in SFr E	BP Net Balance SFr F	EDF Pays to BP FFr G	BP Sells Fwd for SFr in FFr H	BP Pays to FC FFr I	BP Net Balance FFr J
6		4.03		4.03	9.20	5.17	36.42	36.42		0.00
12		4.02		4.02	2.88	4.03	36.42	11.84	24.58	0.00
18		4.03		4.03		0.00	96.50		96.50	0.00
22	5.10					5.10				
24	5.70	4.02	6.78	10.80		0.00	96.50		96.50	0.00
26	5.70					5.70				
28	5.70					11.40				
30	5.70	3.83	13.27	17.10		0.00	96.50		96.50	0.00
32	5.70					5.70				
34	5.70					11.40				
35	5.70					17.10				
36	5.70	3.45	19.35	22.80		0.00	96.50		96.50	0.00
37	5.70					5.70				
38	5.70					11.40				
39	5.70					17.10				
40	5.70					22.80				
41	5.70					28.50				
42	5.70	2.89	31.31	34.20		0.00	96.50		96.50	0.00
43	5.70					5.70				
44	5.70					11.40				
45	5.70					17.10				
47	17.00					34.10				
48		1.99	32.11	34.10		0.00	96.50		96.50	0.00
53	17.00					17.00				
54		1.07	15.93	17.00		0.00	96.50		96.50	0.00
58	22.00					22.00				
60		0.61	21.25	21.86		0.14				

CHAPTER 6

Swap risk analysis

GENERAL

An organisation must understand the risk associated with swap transactions prior to entering into such contractual arrangements, in order to determine whether the cost saving or hedge benefits are worth the additional contractual commitment. With a liability, the insolvency of an investor is of no concern to a borrower. However, if a borrower changes the nature of a liability by the use of a swap (eg, from a fixed-rate dollar liability to a simulated floating-rate dollar liability, or from a fixed-rate Swiss franc liability into a simulated fixed-rate dollar liability), the swap forms a separate obligation. Default by a counterparty may be of substantial financial significance to the borrower, as it may result in a loss. It should be noted, however, that exposure is contingent exposure. If each party performs, there is no exposure. In this sense, exposure is primarily one of credit risk.

Risks under swaps can be broken down into three areas as follows:

documentation risk;
payment risk;
risk of inability to perform.

The documentation risk, or the failure of contract provisions to be upheld or enforced, is dealt with in Chapter 7. The payment, or delivery, risk can be substantially eliminated by the use of escrow paying facilities, also covered in Chapter 7. This chapter examines potential financial exposure which may result from the inability of one of the parties to perform. It also shows a method of calculating precisely, using a hypothetical example, the loss at a particular point in time due to non-performance by one party through, for example, bankruptcy.

Swap risks result from the following factors:

volatility of interest rates;
volatility of exchange rates;
credit standing;
time and probabilities.

The relationship between interest rates and exchange rates is of primary importance. For example, if dollar interest rates were to fall in the US, while interest rates in other countries remained stable, one could expect the dollar to devalue.

Exposure also varies depending on the type of swap transaction entered into. The following table shows the type of exposure for the various forms of swap:

(i) interest rate or coupon swaps, ie, same currency floating-to-fixed swaps	(a) interest exposure on fixed rates
(ii) cross-currency fixed-to-fixed swap	(a) exposure on both currencies (b) Interest exposure on fixed rates

(iii)	cross-currency fixed-to-floating swaps	(a) exposure on both currencies
		(b) interest exposure on fixed-rate currency
(iv)	same currency floating to floating swaps	(a) historical basis risk exposure eg, the yield on 3-month Treasury bills is less than 3-month LIBOR
(v)	cross-currency floating-to-floating swaps	(a) exposure on both currencies

Note: Credit standing, time and probabilities are factors common to all forms of swap.

Because swaps involve so many variables, it is impossible to assess precisely the potential risk under a swap at the time of entering into the transaction. Each swap will have to be individually analysed on a best/worst case basis using historical data as a guide to future volatility. Because of the variables, it is difficult to come up with a meaningful estimate of exposure at the outset of a swap. At best one can make an estimate of exposure based on various assumptions. For example:

— Swiss franc will revalue no more than 35% in the next 5 years
— counterparty will not default during first two years
— dollar fixed-interest rates will not be higher than 16%, or less than 8%, during the life of the swap.

Making such estimates lends itself to statistical analysis using historical data in order to project likely outcomes based on certain probabilities. It is, however, possible to determine precisely the potential loss under a swap due to a default at a particular point in time, because the variables are then known, ie, interest rates, exchange rates and remaining life of the swap.

Exposure can be summarized as the present value of all future amounts to be received, less the present value of all future payments to be made.

To illustrate the different types of exposure under the various forms of swaps, a hypothetical example is considered for the two major forms.*

INTEREST RATE OR COUPON SWAPS

The following is a summary of the approximate terms and conditions of the already discussed Deutsche Bank swap:

Bond issue	Amount:	$110,000,000
	Interest rate:	11%
	Maturity:	7 years
Swap	Notional principal amount:	$110,000,000
	Interest:	
	payments	11% payable annually
	receipts	LIBOR less ¼% payable semi-annually
	Maturity:	7 years

*We are not here discussing the cost of writing a replacement swap on identical terms, which is discussed in Chapter 7, because the cost of any such replacement swap would be determined on the basic principles outlined in this chapter.

If the intermediary defaults, what will be Deutsche's position? Deutsche will still have to make the fixed-rate interest payments to the bondholder, but it will no longer be obliged to make the floating rate payments to the intermediary. Consequently, it will be short fixed-rate payments and long floating-rate payments. The exposure question is easier to understand if we consider what steps Deutsche can take to protect itself. One solution would be for Deutsche to borrow floating-rate finance, as it is long floating-rate interest payments, and with the proceeds buy an 11% US Government Treasury bond such that the income from the bond equals the payments it has to make to the fixed-rate bondholders. Deutsche's exposure (ignoring the opportunity costs) is the difference between the cost of borrowing the floating-rate finance and the floating-rate payments it was due to make under the swap, and the price it has to pay for the Treasury bond less the redemption value of the Treasury bond.

If we assume the market rate for floating-rate finance is always LIBOR (ignoring the $\frac{1}{4}$%), Deutsche only has exposure if the yield on US Treasury bonds falls below 11%. The size of the exposure is dependent on the actual yield on Treasuries at the time of default and the remaining life of the swap.

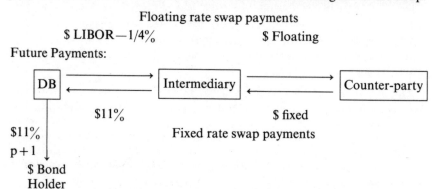

If we make the assumption that seven-year US Treasury bond yields will not fall below $8\frac{1}{2}$% on an annual compounding basis (which in recent times is historically conservative), Deutsche's theoretical exposure is the theoretical price of an 11% seven-year Treasury bond to give a yield of $8\frac{1}{2}$% (112.80), less the redemption value of the Treasury bond (100), or 12.8% (assuming an annual compounding basis). This calculation is made from the following information:

years to maturity	(n)	= 7 years
yields to maturity	(i)	= 8.5%
coupon/interest payment	(PMT)	= 11% .
future value	(FV)	= 100% .
theoretical price of 7-year, 11% US Treasury bond	(PV)	= 112.80
redemption value	(FV)	= 100.00
exposure		12.80

If the intermediary, for simplicity's sake, defaults on day one of the third year (ie, after making its second year payments) and four-year US Treasury bond yields are 9% annual compounding, what would Deutsche's loss be?

In this case, we adjust for the $\frac{1}{4}$% on the LIBOR by assuming the fixed-rate receipt is $11\frac{1}{4}$% and not 11%. By solving for the present value given the following market details, the loss can be assessed.

Notional principal amount		$= \$110,000,000$
Years to maturity	(n)	$= 4$ years
Interest payments	(PMT)	$= 11\frac{1}{4}\%$ $(11\% + \frac{1}{4}\%$ for LIBOR)
Future value	(FV)	$= 100$
Yield to maturity	(i)	$= 9\%$ (current 4-year US Treasury bond yield)
Present value	(PV)	$= 107.29$
Exposure		$=$ PV less FV $\times$ notional principal amount
		$= 107.29\% - 100\% \times 110,000,000$
		$= \$8,019,000$ (equivalent to 7.29% of the notional principal amount)

By examining the above, one can appreciate that Deutsche's exposure only arises if interest rates fall and that, as LIBOR is always assumed to be a market rate, exposure only relates to the fixed-rate interest payments. If interest rates rise, Deutsche has no exposure.

To illustrate the impact that years to maturity have on the calculations, compare the following:

		7 yrs	5 yrs	3 yrs	1 yr
Years to maturity	(n)	7 yrs	5 yrs	3 yrs	1 yr
Interest payment	(PMT)	11%	11%	11%	11%
Future value	(FV)	100%	100%	100%	100%
Theoretical yield to maturity on US Treasury bond	(i)	9%	9%	9%	9%
Theoretical present value of US Treasury bond	(PV)	110.07	107.78	105.06	101.83
Exposure	(PV)−(FV)	10.07%	7.78%	5.06%	1.83%

Thus, exposure calculations revolve entirely around present value concepts and will depend on market conditions prevailing at the time a swap agreement is terminated or closed out. These concepts have now been incorporated into liquidated damages provisions in most swap agreements. The points of most conjecture, of course, are over the discount rates in determining present values. For example, how does one adjust for the $\frac{1}{4}\%$ margin under LIBOR in Deutsche's case? Does one add it to the fixed rate, as we did in the above example? Does one do a separate present value analysis treating the margin as a fixed amount receivable by Deutsche semi-annually? Is it correct to discount the margin at the US Treasury bond rate?

CROSS-CURRENCY FIXED-TO-FIXED SWAPS

It is worthwhile considering exposure under a Type (ii) swap in as much detail as a Type (i) swap. Again it involves present value concepts similar to a coupon or an interest rate swap, the major difference being the impact of foreign currency exposure.

Let us consider the following hypothetical example which considers exposure from the point of view of an intermediary bank which has written two matching currency swaps with two separate counterparties.

Although exposure is considered from an intermediary bank's point of view, the same logic applies in determining a counterparty's exposure.

Hypothetical example

A foreign intermediary bank ('FIB') enters into a seven-year currency exchange agreement ('swap 1') with company A, under which FIB agrees to sell, and A agrees to buy, dollars in the amounts and for the value dates as set out in Schedule A below, in return for A selling to FIB, and FIB agreeing to buy, Swiss francs in the amounts and for the value dates as set out in Schedule B below.

FIB also writes a matching seven-year contract ('swap 2') with company B, under which FIB agrees to sell, and B agrees to buy, Swiss francs in the amounts and for the value dates as set out in Schedule C below, in return for B selling to FIB, and FIB agreeing to buy, dollars in the amounts and for the value dates as set out in Schedule D.

Value Date	*Schedule A* FIB sells to A		*Schedule B* A sells to FIB		*Schedule C* FIB sells to B		*Schedule D* B sells to FIB	
			(all figures in millions)					
Year	$	%	SFr	%	SFr	%	SFRr	%
1 (interest)	5.71	12.00	6.00	6.00	6.00	6.00	5.71	12.00
2 ,,	5.71	12.00	6.00	6.00	6.00	6.00	5.71	12.00
3 ,,	5.71	12.00	6.00	6.00	6.00	6.00	5.71	12.00
4 ,,	5.71	12.00	6.00	6.00	6.00	6.00	5.71	12.00
5 ,,	5.71	12.00	6.00	6.00	6.00	6.00	5.71	12.00
6 ,,	5.71	12.00	6.00	6.00	6.00	6.00	5.71	12.00
7 ,,	5.71	12.00	6.00	6.00	6.00	6.00	5.71	12.00
7 (principal)	47.62	100.00	100.00	100.00	100.00	100.00	47.62	100.00

It is assumed that the exchange rate at the time of entering into both transactions is $1 = SFr 2.10.

This transaction can be depicted as follows.

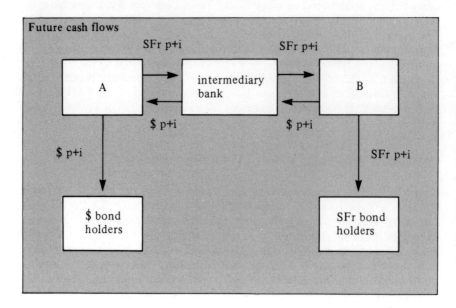

Under the swap agreement, A converts a fixed-rate dollar liability into a simulated fixed-rate Swiss franc liability. The converse applies to B, as B converts a fixed-rate Swiss franc liability into a simulated fixed-rate dollar liability.

If A defaults, the intermediary's obligation would be terminated, and it would claim damages under the agreement. It should be noted that a default does not affect FIB'S contract with B.

As with to the exposure on coupon swaps, the banks exposure is contingent (off-balance sheet) exposure and losses can only arise out of non-performance by one of the parties, or in this example, A. Consequently, exposure is primarily one of credit risk; the actual size of the risk being dependent upon dollar and Swiss franc interest rates, the dollar/Swiss franc exchange rate prevailing at the time of non-performance or default and the remaining life under the swap commitment.

In the event of a default, FIB would still have to perform under its contract with B. FIB's position would be as follows:

(i)	plus $5,710,000 or 12% per annum	(interest)
(ii)	plus $47,620,000 or 100% at maturity	(principal)
(iii)	less SFr 6,000,000 or 6% per annum	(interest)
(iv)	less SFr 100,000,000 or 100% at maturity	(principal)

To protect itself, FIB could take the following course of action on an early termination or close-out:

1. borrow dollars sufficient to buy suitable Swiss franc investment (see 3 below). The cost of borrowing would be matched against the dollar receipts from B;
2. sell dollars spot (at prevailing dollar/Swiss franc exchange rate) for Swiss francs;
3. buy a Swiss franc investment which will generate sufficient future Swiss franc cash flow to make the necessary payments to B.

Based on the above course of action, FIB's exposure can be precisely determined. Exposure under a Type (ii) swap can also be precisely defined as:

The difference between (1) the present value of all the receipts due from the defaulting party; and (2) the present value of all the payments due to the defaulting party.

The extent to which (1) exceeds (2) is FIB's exposure. If (2) is equal to or greater than (1), there is no exposure.

As previously mentioned, assessing exposure under a swap is at best an estimate. Under a Type (i) swap, ie, floating-to-fixed, there is only an exposure on the fixed rate. However, under the above swap, there is exposure on:

(a) both fixed rates, ie, dollars and Swiss francs, and
(b) currencies.

Again other factors also include credit standing, time and probabilities.

Calculations and exposure

When entering into any credit transaction, including a swap, it is reasonable to expect that a party will not default for liquidity reasons during the first two years. If A were to default on the first day in the fourth year of the transaction, based on the following given market data (hypothetical) at that date, exposure under the swap can be precisely calculated:

Market data

	At the time of swap	At the time of default	% change
Market rates			
Maturity	7 years	4 years	
Interest rate – $ (annual)	12.00%	14.00%	16.6
– SFr (annual)	6.00%	4.00%	33.3
Exchange rate	2.12	1.90	10.4

In this example, we have assumed the worst situation for FIB:

(i) dollar (borrowing) rates have increased from 12% to 14%;
(ii) Swiss france (investment) rates have decreased from 6% to 4%; and
(iii) the Swiss franc has revalued from $1 = SFr 2.12 to $1 = SFr 1.90.

This is not an entirely realistic situation, as the interest differential between Swiss francs and dollars has widened from 6% ($12% less SFr 6%) to 10% ($14% less SFr 4%), and the dollar has also devalued. It is important to note the variables, however, and how they each impact the exposure.

Using the logic or format outlined above, exposure can be calculated as follows.

Step 1

Calculate the present value (PV) of the currency (SFr) to be delivered by defaulter (A):

number of years	4	(n)
yield to maturity	4% pa	(i)
interest (coupon)	6% pa	(PMT)
future value	100%	(FV)
present value	107.26%	(PV)

Step 2

Convert the present value (PV) of Swiss francs calculated in Step 1 above, to dollars, using current exchange rate of $1 = SFr 1.90:

present value SFr	107.26	(PV)
exchange rate	$1 = SFr 1.90	
present value	$56.45	(PV)

Step 3

Calculate the present value (PV) of the currency ($) to be delivered to defaulter (A):

number of years	4 years	(n)
yield to maturity	14% annually	(i)
interest (coupon)	12% annually	(PMT)
future value	100%	(FV)
present value	94.17%	(PV)
	or $44.42	(94.17% × $47.17)

Step 4

Calculate the exposure:

present value of receipts	$56.45
present value of payments	$44.42
exposure	$12.03
initial notional principal amount	$47.17
exposure	25.5%

As previously mentioned, the above example assumes for FIB an adverse movement in all the variables. It is important to note, however, the impact each variable can have on the exposure as follows:

    (i) change in Swiss franc rates only (+ or −)
    (ii) change in dollar rates only (+ or −)
    (iii) change in exchange rate only (+ or −)
or (iv) a combination of any of the above (+ or −)

Set out in the Appendix (p. 80 et seq, post) are tables covering the various permutations and combinations involved under Step 4 above, from which can be read the exposure under various scenarios. For example, referring to Table A, one can see if, with four years to run, the dollar/Swiss franc interest rates are the same as the swap, ie, dollars at 12%, Swiss francs at 6%, exposure is entirely related to the currency movement. The positive figures represent exposure for FIB. So, if the currency revalues 10%, reading from the table, there is a 10% exposure. However, if the interest differential widens from 6% to 9%. ie, SFr 4½% to dollars 13½%, and the Swiss franc devalues 5%, the exposure would be only 4.53%. This is a more logical situation, and illustrates how a movement in a favourable direction from FIB's point of view in the currency rates (the Swiss franc devaluation) may offset an adverse movement in Swiss franc interest rates (from 6% to 4½% and dollar rates rising from 12% to 13½%).

Exposure under the various tables apart from Table A which has already been covered above can be summarised as follows:

Table B illustrates how exposure varies as the interest differential changes, given a change only in the dollar interest rates (Swiss franc interest remains constant at 6%) and the Swiss franc devalues and revalues assuming a 4-year maturity;

Table C is the same as Table B, except that the dollar interest rate remains constant at 12% and the Swiss franc interest rate changes;

Table D illustrates how the exposure varies as the maturity (ie, remaining life of the swap) changes, given the Swiss franc and dollar rates for an interest differential of 11% and 1%;

Table E is the same as Table A, except that the maturity is assumed to be five years;

Table F is also the same as Tables A and E, except that the maturity is assumed to be three years;

Table G is also the same as Tables A, E and F, except that the maturity is assumed to be two years.

TABLE A

Table A illustrates how exposure varies as the interest differential changes between Swiss Franc and Dollar rates, and the Swiss Franc devalues and revalues, assuming a 4-year maturity.

SFr	3½	4	4½	5	5½	6	6½	7	7½	8	8½
$	14½	14	13½	13	12½	12	11½	11	10½	10	9½
Int Diff	11	10	9	8	7	6	5	4	3	2	1
Currency SFr											
−25	−10.91	−13.73	−16.55	−19.37	−22.19	−25.00	−27.81	−30.64	−33.47	−36.31	−39.15
−20	−5.45	−8.36	−11.28	−14.19	−17.10	−20.00	−22.90	−25.81	−28.72	−31.64	−34.56
−15	0.01	−3.00	−6.01	−9.01	−12.01	−15.00	−17.98	−20.98	−23.97	−26.97	−29.97
−10	5.47	2.36	−0.74	−3.84	−6.93	−10.00	−13.07	−16.15	−19.22	−22.30	−25.38
−5	10.93	7.73	4.53	1.34	−1.84	−5.00	−8.15	−11.32	−14.47	−17.63	−20.79
0	16.39	13.09	9.80	6.52	3.25	0	−3.24	−6.49	−9.72	−12.96	−16.20
+5	21.85	18.45	15.07	11.70	8.34	5.00	1.68	−1.66	−4.97	−8.29	−11.61
+10	27.31	23.82	20.34	16.88	13.43	10.00	6.59	3.17	−0.22	−3.62	−7.02
+15	32.77	29.18	25.61	22.05	18.51	15.00	11.51	8.00	4.53	1.05	2.43
+20	38.23	34.54	30.88	27.23	23.60	20.00	16.42	12.83	9.28	5.72	2.16
+25	43.69	39.91	36.15	32.41	28.69	25.00	21.33	17.66	14.03	10.39	6.75

Conditions: Swap Rates − SFr   6%

$ 12%

Exch $1 = SFr2.10

Remaining Life − 4 years

TABLE B

Table B illustrates how exposure varies as the interest differential changes, given a change in the Dollar rates (ie Swiss Franc remains constant at 6%), and the Swiss Franc devalues and revalues assuming a 4-year maturity.

SFr	% 6	% 6	% 6	% 6	% 6	% 6	% 6	% 6	% 6	% 6	% 6
$	17	16	15	14	13	12	11	10	9	8	7
Int Diff	11	10	9	8	7	6	5	4	3	2	1
Currency SFr											
−25	−11.28	−13.81	−16.44	−19.17	−22.03	−25.00	−28.10	−31.34	−34.72	−38.25	−41.94
−20	−6.28	−8.81	−11.44	−14.17	−17.03	−20.00	−23.10	−26.34	−29.72	−33.25	−36.94
−15	−1.28	−3.81	−6.44	−9.17	−12.03	−15.00	−18.10	−21.34	−24.72	−28.25	−31.94
−10	3.72	1.19	−1.44	−4.17	−7.03	−10.00	−13.10	−16.34	−19.72	−23.25	−26.94
−5	8.72	6.19	3.56	0.83	−2.03	−5.00	−8.10	−11.34	−14.72	−18.25	−21.94
0	13.72	11.19	8.56	5.83	2.97	0	−3.10	−6.34	−9.72	−13.25	−16.94
+5	18.72	16.19	13.56	10.83	7.97	5.00	1.90	−1.34	−4.72	−8.25	−11.94
+10	23.72	21.19	18.56	15.83	12.97	10.00	6.90	3.66	0.28	−3.25	−6.94
+15	28.72	26.19	23.56	20.83	17.97	15.00	11.90	8.66	5.28	1.75	−1.94
+20	33.72	31.19	28.56	25.83	22.97	20.00	16.90	13.66	10.28	6.75	3.06
+25	38.72	36.19	33.56	30.83	27.97	25.00	21.90	18.66	15.28	11.75	8.06

Conditions: Swap rates – SFr 6%

$ 12%

Exch $1 = SFr 2.10

Remaining life – 4 years

TABLE C

Table C is the same as table B, except that the Dollar rate remains constant at 12%, and the Swiss Franc rate changes.

SFr	%	%	%	%	%	%	%	%	%	%	%
	1	2	3	4	5	6	7	8	9	10	11
$	12	12	12	12	12	12	12	12	12	12	12
Int Diff	11	10	9	8	7	6	5	4	3	2	1
Currency SFr											
−25	−10.37	−13.58	−16.64	−19.56	−22.34	−25.00	−27.54	−29.97	−32.29	−34.51	−36.63
−20	− 4.39	− 7.82	−11.08	−14.19	−17.16	−20.00	−22.71	−25.30	−27.78	−30.14	−32.41
−15	1.58	− 2.05	− 5.52	− 8.83	−11.99	−15.00	−17.88	−20.63	−23.26	−25.78	−28.19
−10	7.56	3.71	0.04	− 3.47	− 6.81	−10.00	−13.05	−15.96	−18.75	−21.41	−23.96
− 5	13.53	9.47	5.59	1.90	− 1.63	− 5.00	− 8.22	−11.29	−14.23	−17.05	−19.74
0	19.51	15.23	11.15	7.26	3.55	0	− 3.39	− 6.62	− 9.72	−12.68	−15.51
+ 5	25.49	20.99	16.71	12.62	8.72	5.00	1.44	− 1.96	− 5.21	− 8.31	−11.29
+10	31.46	26.75	22.27	17.99	13.90	10.00	6.27	2.71	− 0.69	− 3.95	− 7.06
+15	37.44	32.52	27.82	23.35	19.08	15.00	11.10	7.38	3.82	0.42	− 2.84
+20	43.41	38.28	33.38	28.71	24.26	20.00	15.94	12.05	8.34	4.78	1.39
+25	49.39	44.04	38.94	34.07	29.43	25.00	20.77	16.72	12.85	9.15	5.61

Conditions: Swap rates – SFr   6%
                           $ 12%
              Exch $1 = SFr 2.10
              Remaining Life – 4 years

TABLE D

Table D illustrates how the exposure varies as the maturity changes, given the Swiss Franc and Dollar rates for an interest differential of 1½% and 1%.

	SFr 3½%, $14½%, Int Diff 1½%				SFr 8½%, $9½%, Int Diff 1%			
	2 yr	3 yr	4 yr	5 yr	2 yr	3 yr	4 yr	5 yr
−25	−17.25	−13.99	−10.91	− 8.05	−32.69	−36.06	−39.15	−41.99
−20	−12.11	− 8.64	− 5.45	− 2.49	−27.91	−31.38	−34.56	−37.48
−15	− 6.87	− 3.24	0.01	3.08	−23.14	−26.70	−29.97	−32.97
−10	− 1.64	2.06	5.47	8.64	−18.36	−22.02	−25.38	−28.47
− 5	3.60	7.41	10.93	14.21	−13.58	−17.34	−20.79	−23.96
0	8.84	12.76	16.39	19.77	− 8.80	−12.66	−16.20	−19.45
+ 5	14.08	18.11	21.85	25.33	− 4.02	− 7.98	−11.61	−15.94
+10	19.32	23.46	27.31	30.90	0.76	− 3.30	− 7.02	−10.44
+15	24.55	28.81	32.77	36.46	5.54	1.38	− 2.43	− 5.93
+20	29.79	34.16	38.23	42.03	10.31	6.06	2.16	− 1.42
+25	35.03	39.51	43.69	47.59	15.09	10.74	6.95	3.09

TABLE E

Table E is the same as table A, except that the maturity is assumed to be 5 years.

	%	%	%	%	%	%	%	%	%	%	%
SFr	3½	4	4½	5	5½	6	6½	7	7½	8	8½
$	14¼	14	13½	13	12½	12	11½	11	10½	10	9½
Int Diff	11	10	9	8	7	6	5	4	3	2	1
Currency SFr											
−25	−8.05	−11.46	−14.86	−18.24	−21.62	−25	−28.38	−31.77	−35.17	−38.57	−41.99
−20	−2.49	−6.04	−9.52	−13.02	−16.51	−20	−23.49	−26.98	−30.47	−33.97	−37.48
−15	3.08	−0.57	−4.19	−7.08	−11.40	−15	−18.59	−22.18	−25.77	−29.37	−32.97
−10	8.64	4.98	1.14	−2.59	−6.30	−10	−13.69	−17.39	−21.08	−24.77	−28.47
−5	14.21	10.32	6.47	2.63	−1.19	−5	−8.80	−12.59	−16.38	−20.17	−23.96
0	19.77	15.77	11.80	7.85	3.92	0	−3.90	−7.80	−11.68	−15.57	−19.45
+5	25.33	21.21	17.13	13.06	9.02	5	.99	−3.00	−6.99	−10.97	−14.94
+10	30.90	26.66	22.46	18.28	14.13	10	5.89	1.79	−2.29	−6.37	−10.44
+15	36.46	32.11	27.78	23.50	19.24	15	10.79	6.59	42.41	−1.76	5.93
+20	42.03	37.55	33.11	28.71	24.34	20	15.68	11.38	7.10	2.84	1.42
+25	47.59	43.00	38.44	33.93	29.45	25	20.58	16.18	11.80	7.44	3.09

Conditions: Swap rates – SFr   6%
$ 12%
Exch $1 = SFr 2.10
Remaining Life – 5 years

TABLE F

Table F is also the same as table A and table E, except that the maturity is assumed to be 3 years.

	% 3½ 14½ 11	% 4 14 10	% 4½ 13½ 9	% 5 13 8	% 5½ 12½ 7	% 6 12 6	% 6½ 11½ 5	% 7 11 4	% 7½ 10½ 3	% 8 10 2	% 8½ 9½ 1
SFr $ Int Diff											
Currency SFr											
−25	−13.99	−16.19	−18.40	−20.60	−22.80	−25	−27.20	−29.41	−31.62	−33.84	−36.06
−20	−8.64	−10.92	−13.19	−15.46	−17.73	−20	−22.27	−24.54	−26.32	−29.10	−31.38
−15	−3.29	−5.46	−7.98	−10.32	−12.66	−15	−17.34	−19.67	−22.01	−24.35	−26.70
−10	2.06	−0.36	−2.78	−5.19	−7.60	−10	−12.40	−14.81	−17.21	−19.61	−22.02
−5	7.41	4.92	2.43	.05	−2.53	−5	−7.47	−9.94	−12.40	−14.87	−17.34
0	12.76	10.19	7.64	5.08	2.54	0	−2.54	−5.07	−7.60	−10.13	−12.66
+5	18.11	15.47	12.84	10.22	7.61	5	2.40	.20	−2.79	−5.39	−7.98
+10	23.46	20.75	18.05	15.36	12.67	10	7.33	4.67	2.01	.64	−3.30
+15	28.81	26.03	23.25	20.49	17.74	15	12.27	9.54	6.32	4.10	1.38
+20	34.16	31.03	28.46	25.63	22.81	20	17.20	14.41	11.62	8.84	6.06
+25	39.51	36.58	33.67	30.77	27.88	25	22.13	19.28	16.43	13.58	10.74

Conditions: Swap rates – SFr 6%
$ 12%
Exch $1 = SFr 2.10
Remaining Life 3 years

TABLE G

Table G is also the same as tables A, E and F, except that the maturity is assumed to be 2 years.

SFr	3½	4	4½	5	5½	6	6½	7	7½	8	8½
$	14½	14	13½	13	12½	12	11½	11	10½	10	9½
Int Diff	11	10	9	8	7	6	5	4	3	2	1
Currency SFr											
−25	−17.35	−18.88	−20.41	−21.94	−23.47	−25	−26.53	−28.07	−29.61	−31.15	−32.69
−20	−12.11	−13.69	−15.27	−16.84	−18.42	−20	−21.58	−23.16	−24.74	−26.32	−27.91
−15	−6.87	−8.50	−10.13	−11.75	−13.38	−15	−16.62	−18.25	−19.38	−21.50	−23.14
−10	−1.64	−3.31	−4.99	−6.66	−8.33	−10	−11.67	−13.34	−15.01	−16.68	−18.36
−5	3.60	1.88	.15	−1.57	−3.28	−5	−6.72	−8.43	−10.14	−11.86	−13.58
0	8.84	7.07	5.24	3.53	1.76	0	−1.76	−3.52	−5.28	−7.04	−8.80
+5	14.08	12.25	10.44	8.62	6.81	5	3.19	1.39	.41	−2.22	−4.02
+10	19.32	17.44	15.58	13.71	11.85	10	8.15	6.30	4.45	2.61	0.76
+15	24.55	22.63	20.72	18.81	16.90	15	13.10	11.21	9.32	7.43	5.54
+20	29.79	27.82	25.86	23.90	21.95	20	18.06	16.12	14.18	12.25	10.31
+25	35.03	33.01	31.00	28.99	26.99	25	23.01	21.03	19.05	17.07	15.09

Conditions: Swap rates – SFr   6%
$ 12%

Exch $1 = SFr 2.10

Remaining Life – 2 years

CHAPTER 7

Standard documentation

Documentation for swap transactions ranges from four to thirty or more pages long. Occasionally the added length reflects particular credit considerations or additional complexities such as syndication or guarantees, but more often the length is the result of the draftsman's style and the client's expectations. The typical interest or currency swap agreement would be approximately twelve pages, although there has been a recent trend to longer documentation. This chapter will present a standard form* of currency swap agreement between a corporate party and an intermediary bank (using fixed-rate Swiss francs payable by the bank and LIBOR-based dollars payable by the company) and discuss documentation and related legal issues section by section. In addition, where typical interest swap provisions would be drafted in a significantly different conceptual manner than in a currency swap, the interest swap provisions will be set out separately, with the fixed rate amount payable by the bank and the floating-rate, or variable, amount payable by the company.

PARTIES AND STRUCTURE

The nature of the parties and their respective reasons for entering into the swap agreement may have an effect on specific provisions throughout the agreement. Two points, timing of effectiveness and presence of an intermediary bank, will be mentioned at the outset.

Timing

The assets or liabilities being hedged may result in exposure gaps on execution. For instance, assume an interest swap with a new LIBOR borrower on one side and a new fixed rate bond issuer on the other. The bond issuer would want the counterparty irrevocably committed on the launch of the bond issue, with a possible condition precedent to effectiveness of the swap that the bonds actually be issued. The LIBOR borrower, however, has conditions precedent to its right to borrow and it must give an irrevocable borrowing notice two to five business days before borrowing. Thus, it would want the other party irrevocably committed no later than the date of the borrowing notice, possibly with a condition precedent that the loan actually be made. There is no solution to this timing problem without at least one party, or perhaps an intermediary bank, taking the risk of failure of conditions in the bond issue or borrowing.

Intermediary

If one of the parties is an intermediary bank, there are certain drafting changes often present on what might be called the 'intermediary theory'.

* In the form, items in square brackets indicate alternate preferences.

This argument, not always successful, is based on two principles. First, the intermediary is acting as a conduit. In entering into the transaction, the intermediary's function is to take the credit risk of the two parties, but not risks incident to changes of law and taxes. Any such change which reduces a payment it receives or increases a payment it must make destroys its spread. This is analogous to typical cost-plus eurodollar financing. Second, banks customarily require certain covenants and events of default from corporate parties in credit transactions, while corporate parties do not require them from the bank (compare a loan agreement with a certificate of deposit).

Application of the intermediary theory has a number of ramifications in drafting, some of which will be pointed out in the course of discussing documentation.

RECITALS

Typically, the agreement will commence with recitals indicating the reason for which the parties are entering into the transaction. Recitals are important for two primary reasons.

First, without such recitals, or without the facts set forth in the recitals, there is a perceived risk that swap agreements might violate gaming or gambling statutes of various jurisdictions. New York's gambling statute renders gambling contracts unenforceable. The typical interest or currency swap entered into for the typical reason does not violate this statute, because of the commercial interests of the parties in the future contingent events. Various firms of solicitors have rendered conflicting opinions as to the risk, theoretical or otherwise, under the English gaming laws, although the clear majority view by now is that typical swap agreements are not gaming contracts under English laws. Under Australian law, swaps have traditionally been structured as mutual indemnity contracts to avoid the Australian gaming laws. Finally, some German entities tend to write their contracts through off-shore affiliates because of their view that, regardless of recitals, there are gaming act risks under German law. The recitals, by emphasising the commercial interests of the parties, serve to rebut inferences that the agreement is a gaming contract.

Second, recitals which emphasise the nature of the transaction also are helpful in supporting enforcement. By emphasising the nature of the assets or liabilities being hedged, the parties indicate on the face of the agreement the nature of losses which would be incurred on an early termination. In addition, if the agreement can be successfully characterised as a 'financial accommodation' in a US insolvency proceeding, the enforcing party may have certain advantages in the insolvency of the other party. These issues are discussed in greater detail below.

Typical heading and recitals would be as shown opposite:

DEFINITIONS

The definitions invariably include business day, currency or currencies which are relevant, the amounts to be exchanged, including definitions of rates used, and payment dates. Definitions of payment dates and business days relating to the different payments often depend on the structure of the

CURRENCY EXCHANGE AGREEMENT

THIS CURRENCY EXCHANGE AGREEMENT is made ....
198 ... between ...., a bank
organized under the laws of .... and acting
through its .... branch (herein called 'the Bank'),
and ...., a
[corporation organized] [company incorporated] under the laws of
....(herein called 'the Company').

WHEREAS, the Company has certain Swiss franc obligations
bearing interest at a fixed rate per annum and certain dollar assets and
the Company desires to reduce the exchange and interest risks incident
thereto; and

WHEREAS, the Bank has made or proposes to make arrangements
satisfactory to it to effect one or more transactions, substantially the
reverse of the arrangements embodied in this Agreement, with at least
one other counterparty which has incurred, or expects to incur, Dollar
obligations at a floating rate per annum but which desires, because of its
sources of revenues and funding, that its obligations effectively be in
Swiss francs at a fixed rate per annum and, accordingly, the Bank is
prepared to extend to the Company the financial accommodation herein
provided;

NOW THEREFORE

IN CONSIDERATION of the mutual agreements hereinafter set
forth, the Bank and the Company agree as follows:

assets and liabilities in the background of the transaction. For example, if
a bond issue is being matched with a LIBOR borrowing, the fixed payment
is usually made by the issuer to the fiscal agent annually on the day before
the actual due date and the floating rate payment is usually made semi-
annually on the actual due date. Where different currencies are involved,
simultaneous payment dates must be a business day in the principal financial centres of the jurisdiction of both currencies. The occasional odd interest period in one market may then result: a LIBOR interest period may be
in effect for, eg, five months and twenty-eight days, with a consequent
minor effect on the rate obtainable. This problem is sometimes resolved by
specifying in the definition of LIBOR a six-month period rather than referring to actual number of days in the variable interest period.

If one of the payments is based on a fixed rate, it will usually be defined
as a flat amount, as if it were on a coupon basis.

The floating rate may be based on a rate such as prime, Treasury bill
auction rates or commercial paper rates which may change during the
calculation period. In this case, the variable amount would generally be
defined as the amount of interest which would accrue on a daily basis
during the relevant period at the rate as from time to time in effect. If the
variable rate is one that is reset at specified intervals and is based on interim
periods shorter than the calculation period, the variable amount may be the

result of compounded interest obtained by adding to the notional principal amount accruals prior to each interim period. There may be margins, above or below the floating rate, or the floating rate may be based on an administered rate (such as the prime rate) which has a margin over cost of funds built into it; this presents minor drafting issues throughout, including on early close-out, but will not hereafter be mentioned.

If the floating rate is based on LIBOR or another variable rate which is constant over the interest period, the variable amount is usually defined as the product of the notional principal amount, the variable rate in effect during the given period and a fraction equal to the number of days in such period over a 360 (dollar) or 365 (sterling) day year. The definition of LIBOR is generally based on quotations from specified reference banks. There has been recent discussion regarding the use of publicly quoted rates, such as those found in specified editions of respected financial dailies or on the Reuters screen, in order to obtain a more readily available quote, to avoid disputes over choice of reference banks and to avoid reference bank fees or agreements which are sometimes required. If the determination process does not result in a quote, there are generally fallback provisions, the LIBOR 'cascade', which would first look to alternate sources of London interbank pricing and then look to the cost of dollars in other jurisdictions, such as New York. Most agreements will provide that, if none of the methods result in a quotation, a recent rate will be used. A few agreements provide that, failing a quote obtained by specified methods, the agreement would terminate.

Periodic amortisation, if any, of the principal amounts in a currency swap can be effected through definitions of the payment amounts and the notional principal amounts, by increasing the relevant payments on certain payment dates by the amounts of notional principal deemed amortised and simultaneously reducing the defined notional principal amounts by the corresponding figure. Amortisation in an interest swap can be effected by periodically decreasing the defined notional principal amount.

As a matter of style, definitions relating to close-out are often relegated either to the close-out section or to an appendix, in order not to disrupt the flow of the document. (See pp. 91 and 92.)

EXCHANGES

The next section would typically be the central section of the agreement, providing for exchanges. It usually provides that on a settlement date, if two currencies are involved, each party pays its required amount to the other party. Occasionally, an agreement with a bank intermediary may include an obligation on it to pay only to the extent funds are received by the bank under the matching agreement. On analysis, this is analogous to the sale of a non-recourse participation in a loan.

If, in a currency swap, there is to be an exchange of currencies on the Effective Date, it can be provided as a separate section under this Article. (See p. 93.)

In an interest swap with same day settlement, there is usually a comparison of the two payments and the appropriate party pays the excess to the other, although this may somewhat increase the theoretical risk under various gaming statutes. (See p. 93.)

It is obviously safer from a credit point of view if payment dates are the same on both sides so that all payments are conditional, one against the

ARTICLE I
DEFINITIONS

Section 1.01. Definitions   As used in this Agreement, terms defined elsewhere herein (including without limitation Schedule A) shall have the meanings there specified and the following terms shall have the following meanings (such meanings to be equally applicable to both the singular and plural forms of the terms defined):

(*a*)   *Accelerated Settlement Date* means the date designated as such pursuant to Section 5.01;

(*b*)   *Business Day* means a day on which banks and foreign exchange markets are open for the transaction of business required for this Agreement in New York City, Zurich and London;

(*c*)   *Dollar Amount* with respect to a given Settlement Date means the product in Dollars of (i) the Dollar Principal Amount, (ii) LIBOR for the Interest Period ending on such given Settlement Date and (iii) a fraction, the numerator of which is the number of days in such Interest Period and the denominator of which is 360, plus, in the case of the last scheduled Settlement Date, the Dollar Principal Amount;

(*d*)   *Dollar Principal Amount* means $ ....;

(*e*)   *Dollars* or the sign $ means lawful currency of the United States of America for the time being and, in relation to all payments in Dollars hereunder, same day funds through the New York Clearing House Interbank Payments System or such other funds as shall from time to time be customary for the settlement of international payments denominated in Dollars;

(*f*)   *Effective Date* means [...................., 198 ....] [the date of this Agreement];

(*g*)   *Event of Default* means one of the events set forth in Section 5.01 (a);

(*h*)   *Interest Period* means each period from and including one Settlement Date (or, with respect to the first Interest Period, the Effective Date) to the next following Settlement Date;

(*i*)   *LIBOR* means, for any period, the rate determined by the Reference Bank as the rate per annum at which its principal London office* was offered deposits in Dollars as of 11:00 a.m. (London time) on the day (herein called the 'Determination Date') two Business Days prior to the first day of such period by prime banks in the London interbank market for delivery on the first day of such period and for the number of days in such period, in an amount comparable to [the Dollar Principal Amount] [$10,000,000]**. However, if such deposits are not so offered to the Reference Bank, 'LIBOR' for such period shall be the rate per annum which the Reference Bank determines to be

---

* Often, several Reference Banks will be used, in which case a 'Reference Agent' is designated to collect the quotations and make the other relevant calculations under the Agreement.
** Occasionally, the parties will agree a mutually acceptable, readily available amount for calculation of LIBOR regardless of actual Dollar Principal Amount.

(i) equal to the arithmetic mean (rounded up, if necessary, to the nearest .....%) of the best rates at which the principal London offices of ...., ... and .... (herein called 'Alternate Banks') were offered deposits in Dollars as of 11:00 a.m. (London time) on such Determination Date by prime banks in the London interbank market for delivery on the first day of such period and for the number of days in such period, in an amount comparable to [the Dollar Principal Amount] [$10,000,000];

or, in the event that the Reference Bank can determine no such arithmetic mean,

(ii) equal to the best fixed Dollar lending rates which the principal New York offices of the Alternate Banks are quoting in New York City as of 11:00 a.m. (New York City time) on such Determination Date to [the New York City branches of leading European] [prime] banks for such period in an amount comparable to [the Dollar Principal Amount] [$10,000,000];

or, if the Alternate Banks are not quoting as mentioned above,

(iii) equal to LIBOR in effect on the nearest day, prior to the first day of such period, for which LIBOR can be determined by the Reference Bank;

(*j*)   *Payment Dates* means the Settlement Dates and the Accelerated Settlement Date;

(*k*)   *Reference Bank* means the Bank or, if an Event of Default shall have occurred and be continuing with respect to the Bank, ... or if ....shall fail to perform the function of Reference Bank hereunder, such other bank with offices in London and New York City as the parties shall agree;

(*l*)   *Settlement Dates* means the ....day of .... [and ....] of each year, commencing ...., 19..... and terminating with the Termination Date;*

(*m*)   *Swiss Franc Amount* with respect to a given Settlement Date means SF....................., plus, in the case of the last scheduled Settlement Date, the Swiss Franc Principal Amount;

(*n*)   *Swiss Franc Principal Amount* means SF ....;

(*o*)   *Swiss Francs* or the sign *SF* means lawful currency of Switzerland for the time being and, in relation to all payments in Swiss Francs hereunder, ...; and

(*p*)   *Termination Date* means ...., 19.....

* If payment schedules are different (eg, dollars paid semi-annually and Swiss francs annually), changes must be made.

ARTICLE II
EXCHANGES

[Currency Swap]

Section 2.01. Delivery of Currencies On each Settlement Date, subject to the terms and conditions contained in this Agreement, the Bank agrees to pay the Swiss Franc Amount for such Settlement Date to the Company and the Company agrees to pay the Dollar Amount for such Settlement Date to the Bank, each such payment to be in consideration of the other payment.

other, or, if in the same currency, netted off against each other with only the excess paid. Netting out also has the advantage of reducing or eliminating payments which might be subject to withholding tax. If, however, a floating-rate amount is being matched against a fixed-rate amount the former is often payable on a semi-annual basis and the latter on an annual basis. This does present some exposure. That exposure can, if desired, be eliminated by re-deploying the variable amount for the second six-month period in the annual period so that in effect all payments are made annually. This is, however, generally not done.

Many agreements also contain a provision that not only are payments on a given settlement date conditional against each other (see section 5.04(a) below) but that, in addition, a party owing an amount on a settlement date would not be obligated to make its payment if at that time there were any amounts owing to it by the other party which had not been paid or tendered.

DETAILS OF PAYMENTS

The next Article typically sets out the particular provisions applicable to payments. A section will state where payments are to be made. Occasionally, if different currencies are involved and due to the time difference between the relevant financial centres, parties will establish complex escrow arrangements with a bank, or even more complex arrangements with two

[Interest Swap]

Section 2.01. Settlement Date Payments On the second Business Day before each Settlement Date, the Reference Bank shall determine the difference between the Fixed Amount for such Settlement Date and the Variable Amount for such Settlement Date. If, as so determined, such Fixed Amount is greater than such Variable Amount, the Bank on such Settlement Date shall pay the difference to the Company; if, as so determined, such Variable Amount is greater than such Fixed Amount, the Company on such Settlement Date shall pay the difference to the Bank; and if, as so determined, there is no such difference, the parties will be deemed to have performed their relevant obligations on such Settlement Date for purposes of this Section 2.01 without any payment having to be made.

banks, in order to eliminate the payment risk. These provisions would require that one party pay its required amount to a bank in escrow for payment on the appropriate date if the other party has paid its amount to that or a different bank in escrow for payment to the first party on that day. This is the safest from a credit point of view, but the party paying dollars basically has to move its money into the escrow bank the preceding business day so that payments can be made by an appropriate time in London, Zurich or Paris, as the case may be. The complicated system is sometimes avoided by giving a party the right to request such a system if it deems necessary for credit purposes or to provide that a party receiving an amount will be deemed to hold a comparable amount in trust for the other until it has made its payment. This latter provision may or may not be enforceable, but it is not prejudicial and it does marginally increase the comfort level of the parties.

ARTICLE III
PAYMENTS

Section 3.01. (*a*) *Place and Time.* Payments shall be effected on the Payment Dates as follows:

(i) The Company shall pay the required amount in Dollars to the Bank at the principal New York City office of [..................................] [the Bank] located at the date hereof at ...., New York, New York ...., USA by 10:00 a.m. New York time; and

(ii) The Bank shall pay the required amount in Swiss Francs to the Company at the Zurich office of [............................] [the Bank], located at the date hereof at .... by .... .m. Zurich time.

(*b*) *Holding in Trust and Escrow.* If either party shall receive an amount in Swiss Francs or an amount in Dollars before the other party receives the corresponding amount in Dollars or the corresponding amount in Swiss Francs, the receiving party shall hold an amount comparable to that so received in trust for the benefit of the other party until such time as the other party receives the amount due to be received by it. [If by reason of the time difference between New York City and Zurich, it is not possible for simultaneous payments to be made, the Bank* may at its option and in its sole discretion notify the Company that payments on a given Payment Date are to be made in escrow. In this case deposits shall be made with [..............................] [the Reference Bank] (in Dollars by the Company in New York City and in Swiss Francs by the Bank in Zurich) prior to .... .m. Zurich time on the applicable Payment Date, in each case accompanied by irrevocable payment instructions to effect the payments required by Section 2.01 or 5.03, as the case may be, payment of each of which deposits shall be conditional only on receipt by [..........................] [the Reference Bank] of the other deposits accompanied by such irrevocable payment instructions so conditioned.]

Another provision would address the movement of a payment date if it otherwise would fall on a day other than a business day. In deciding whether to move payment forward or backward in the event that a settlement date is not a business day, attention should be paid to the underlying

---

* Being the Swiss franc, ie, earlier, payor.

rights and obligations which are being hedged. For instance, in a **LIBOR** borrowing, the payment date would typically be deferred unless it would move into the next calendar month in which case it would be brought forward and interest would be calculated accordingly; in a Eurobond issue, the payment date would be brought forward, but the coupon would remain unchanged; and in a fixed-rate certificate of deposit or US fixed-rate borrowing, the payment date would in effect be deferred, regardless of it being the month end, and interest would remain unchanged. The different effects of a payment date falling on a non-business day are often provided for in the definitions of the fixed settlement date and the variable settlement date or there can be a separate provision as follows:

> **Section 3.02. Payment on Business Days.** If a Settlement Date shall fall on a day which is not a Business Day, such Settlement Date shall be postponed to the next succeeding Business Day [*provided* that, if such next succeeding Business Day falls in another calendar month, such Settlement Date shall be the immediately preceding Business Day].

A judgement currency clause is typically included in currency swaps or cross-border interest swaps which is similar to that customarily found in loan agreements. As with similar provisions in loan agreements, enforcement of judgement currency clauses may be subject to question in some jurisdictions. Nonetheless, it is useful and advisable to include a clause as follows:

> **Section 3.03. Payment in Currency of Obligation.** It is of the essence of this Agreement that the respective parties make the various payments hereunder in the currencies expressed (the currency expressed with respect to each payment herein called the 'required currency' of such payment). The obligation of each party to make each payment in the required currency shall not be discharged or satisfied by any tender, or any recovery pursuant to any judgment, which is expressed in or converted into any other currency until and except to the extent such tender or recovery shall result in the actual receipt by the receiving party in the required currency of the amount expressed to be payable in that currency. The obligation of each party to make payments in the required currency shall be enforceable as an alternative or additional cause of action for the purpose of recovery in the required currency of the amount (if any) by which such actual receipt shall fall short of the full amount of the required currency and shall not be affected by judgment being obtained for any other sums due under this Agreement.

Taxes

A party's view on the withholding tax provision of an agreement should be formed after analysis of the tax laws of the jurisdiction in which it is incorporated and, if different, the jurisdiction through which it is acting and the relevant jurisdictions for its counterparty. Some jurisdictions have higher risks of withholding tax than other jurisdictions. Risks are based on both local statutes (ie, is a tax imposed?) and treaty (ie, if imposed, is there treaty exemption?). If one party is in a low risk jurisdiction and the other party is in a high risk jurisdiction, the first party will clearly want a clause requiring gross-up in the event that withholding taxes become applicable. The second party's preference would be no tax clause, with the effect that if a party becomes obligated to withhold taxes, it may do so, pay such taxes to the appropriate government, and pay only the reduced remaining amount directly to the counterparty. The low risk jurisdictions are those in which there are generally no withholding taxes applied on payments overseas. We have been advised that under present law, for example, the tax statutes of Panama, the Netherlands Antilles and Luxembourg do not impose withholding taxes on most overseas payments, including typical swap payments. If one party is a banking intermediary, the tax section may be one-sided, in that the corporate party would pay free and clear of taxes to the bank but the intermediary would pay net of any taxes.

The taxing authorities of few, if any, jurisdictions which generally impose withholding on overseas payments have taken a public position on the treatment of swap payments for purposes of application of their tax withholding laws. Thus, there is a great deal of uncertainty, which uncertainty precludes discussion of the tax laws of a number of countries*.

Under current US tax laws,** swap payments between two US corporations, including banks and their foreign branches, will not be subject to US withholding tax since payments of any sort between two US corporations are currently not subject to any US withholding tax. The United States does, however, impose, subject to certain exceptions, a 30% withholding tax on US source dividends, interest, premiums, annuities, compensation and other 'fixed or determinable annual or periodical gains, profits and income' which are received by a non-US person and are not 'effectively connected' with a trade or business conducted by that person within the United States. Since the US tax authorities have not yet indicated how they will analyse interest swap payments made by a US party to a non-US party, there is always some risk of tax being imposed. It is unlikely that interest swap payments would be regarded as interest payments and thus subject to the US withholding tax. Thus, the recent changes in US tax laws eliminating withholding tax on certain overseas payments of interest will not affect the tax treatment of swap payments.

Despite these uncertainties, it can be argued, based on the limited available authority and in particular the policy and purpose underlying the 'fixed or determinable annual or periodical' income concept and the US source-of-income rules, that the income realised by a non-US party in connection with an interest rate swap payment from a US party should not be subject to US withholding tax both because such income should ordinarily be treated as non-US source income and because such income should not be considered 'fixed or determinable annual or periodical' income. As a matter of general, but long-standing and vigorous, US tax policy, an item of income is not considered a 'fixed or determinable annual or periodical' item of income unless it contains a high ratio of net income to gross income. An analogy would be to insurance premium payments, which consist of an unquantifiable element representing future losses. To impose a withholding tax on the full amount of such a payment would inequitably result in a tax on gross income rather than net. It thus can be argued that most swap

---

* It is understood that, at the time of writing, the US Internal Revenue Service is considering the nature of swaps for purposes of the US tax laws.

** This summarises, very briefly, Belmore, 'Are Swap Payments Subject to US Withholding Tax?' *International Financial Law Review*, February 1984, to which reference should be made for a fuller analysis.

payments (whether made net or gross) should be analysed as having neither a high ratio nor a relatively constant ratio of net income to gross income, since the next settlement date may require different payment flows due to market changes. It also can be argued that the income realised by a non-US party in connection with a swap payment from a US party should ordinarily be treated as non-US source income for purposes of US withholding tax.

Finally, even if swap payments were ultimately analysed as a type of payment subject to statutory withholding, additional arguments against the application of US withholding would normally be available to the extent the foreign recipient was incorporated in a country that was party to a US income tax treaty. Income tax treaties typically provide that the 'industrial and commercial' profits of an entity of one country will be exempt from tax by the other country, provided those profits are not attributable to a 'permanent establishment' located in the other country. For this purpose, it is likely, although not completely certain, that a swap payment would be considered part of the 'industrial and commercial' profits of the recipient and would accordingly be shielded by the relevant tax treaty from US withholding tax to the extent the recipient did not have a US permanent establishment to which such payment was attributable. If the payment is attributable to that establishment, the payment is not subject to withholding tax since the payee is liable for taxes directly in the US.

The UK position appears to be equally complicated. On a statutory and case law analysis, it appears that swap payments would not be regarded as interest. The concern would be that swap payments are regarded as 'annual payments'. Again, the theory is that they constitute pure profit in the hands of the recipient. The Inland Revenue has issued a private written interpretation to the effect that while swap payments are annual payments, if made to or by a recognised bank in the UK they will not be subject to withholding but are so subject if such a bank is not involved. It is important to note, however, that under the terms of this interpretation the Inland Revenue takes the view that payments made by a bank acting as a principal in an interest rate swap agreement may in certain circumstances be non-tax deductible. This interpretation could, of course, be withdrawn at any time. If treated as annual payments, swap payments made by a non-bank UK party to a foreign party not effectively connected to the latter's UK business may, as in the case of a US party as discussed above, be shielded by the relevant tax treaty, although such payments will not, in strictness, be tax deductible for the payer, unless a non-discrimination article of the relevant tax treaty gives protection. If such payments constitute an annual payment, withholding would be applicable on a payment by an English company to an English company. If the agreement was between the English branch of a foreign bank and a non-UK company, the agreement was governed by foreign law and the agreement was held off-shore, the payments could be regarded as off-shore income and off-shore payments not subject to withholding, but then questions would arise as to the branch's right to deduct such payments as a charge on income.

A typical tax clause would be as shown on p. 98.

There would typically be one or two additional clauses relating to taxes. The first would provide that, if taxes did become deductible on a payment under the swap agreement, the parties would negotiate in good faith to determine whether or not one of them could change its relevant office in order to avoid such taxes. This can be drafted in several ways, ranging from

> **Section 3.04. Payments Free of Taxes.**   Payments hereunder shall be made without any set-off or counterclaim (other than by reason of the recipient failing to deliver a required amount under Section 2.01 or 5.03, as the case may be) and without any restriction or condition and shall be made free and clear of, and without deduction or withholding for or on account of, any Taxes. As used herein, 'Taxes' includes any present or future tax, excise or other taxes of whatever nature (other than taxes generally assessed on the overall net income of the recipient by the jurisdiction of incorporation of the recipient and of the location of the branch through which it is acting hereunder) now or hereafter imposed by any governmental or other authority as well as all levies, imposts, duties, charges or fees of whatever nature. If a party is required by law to deduct or withhold Taxes on any such payment, it will pay to the recipient such additional amount as may be necessary in order that the net amount received by the recipient after the required deduction or withholding (including any required deduction and withholding on such additional amount) shall equal the amount the recipient would have received had no such deduction or withholding been made. Each party will deliver such official forms as the other may reasonably request with respect to tax matters, *provided* that neither party shall be obligated to prejudice its interests thereby.

a short clause to a much more complicated system of notices of change, periods in which to object, notices of objection based on material prejudice and requests for the other party to change its office, starting the process over again.

> **Section 3.05. Negotiations for Change of Office.**   If either party is obligated to make a payment under Section 3.04 then, without prejudice to the obligation of such party to make each such payment when it falls due, the Company and the Bank shall negotiate to determine whether the arrangements set out in this Agreement may be modified (including consideration of a change in relevant office and substituting in the place of a party hereto an entity incorporated or doing business in another jurisdiction) in order to reduce or eliminate the extra cost for the party making such payment, *provided* that this Section 3.05 shall not impose on the other party any obligation other than to negotiate in good faith.

In addition, there is often a provision to close out the agreement in the event tax withholding applies. Sometimes this is treated in the same manner as if it were an event of default with respect to the party closing out for such a reason, on the theory that such treatment will serve as an incentive to the relevant party to devise means to avoid the tax. This provision is set forth below under the discussion of termination provisions.

WARRANTIES, COVENANTS AND CONDITIONS

The next major Article would typically deal with warranties. (See p. 99.) The warranties generally are a scaled down version of those customarily found in loan agreements. They tend to be mutual and relate to due authorisation, to compliance with applicable laws, other agreements and constituent documents and to financial statements, although intermediary banks rarely warrant the latter. Covenants are again generally the most basic, usually only providing for maintenance of appropriate approvals and notification of events of default. In addition, a corporate counterparty usually would agree to deliver periodic financial statements to a bank intermediary, since most banks would be required to maintain current credit files on their customers.

ARTICLE IV
WARRANTIES AND COVENANTS

Section 4.01. Warranties and Covenants. To induce the other to enter into this Agreement, each party warrants and covenants with respect to itself that:

(*a*)   It is, in the case of the Bank, a bank duly existing under the laws of ....and, in the case of the Company, a [corporation] [company] duly existing under the laws of ....;

(*b*)   It is duly authorized to execute, deliver and perform this Agreement;

(*c*)   The execution, delivery and performance of this Agreement do not conflict with any provision of law or of its constitutive documents or of any agreement binding upon it;

(*d*)   All necessary consents, licenses, approvals and authorizations of and registrations or declarations with any governmental or regulatory authority required in connection with its execution, delivery and performance of this Agreement have been obtained, are in full force and effect and shall be maintained together with any additional consents, licenses, approvals, authorizations, registrations or declarations which become necessary in connection therewith, and it shall comply in all material respects with the terms of each thereof; and

(*e*)   No Event of Default (without regard to any provision requiring the lapse of time or giving of notice or both) with respect to it has occurred and is continuing, and it will notify the other, promptly upon it becoming aware of any such event.

[Bank may consider additional warranties and covenants applicable to Company]

Some agreements contain clauses providing for conditions precedent. Other agreements are silent on this issue, and the parties set forth the conditions in a separate closing memorandum, providing for exchange of documents on signing. The theory behind the first approach is that swap agreements typically close on short notice and, if the requirement to exchange closing documents is not set forth in the agreement, no obligation arises to deliver them subsequently. The theory behind the latter approach is that, once signed, parties do not wish any ambiguities as to mutual obligations. In a loan transaction, conditions are one-sided: if they are not satisfied, the borrower does not get its money; if they are satisfied, it does. The ambiguities are resolved at an early stage. In a swap, potential defences based on unsatisfied conditions may well create difficulties at a later date. A solution to the latter problem is to couch the requirement for delivery of the closing documents as an obligation rather than a condition.

In a swap between two banks, the parties often do not provide for closing documents on the theory that they are acting on a bank-to-bank basis in the normal course of their respective businesses. Even then, if the banks are in different jurisdictions, one or both might require an attorneys' opinion as to the laws of the relevant jurisdiction.

> **Section 4.02.   Closing Documents.**   Each party agrees to deliver to the other [on or before] [within .... days after] the Effective Date, the following documents:
>
> [Specify documents, eg, certified resolutions, charter and by-laws, certificate of incumbency, lawyer's opinion]

TERMINATION PROVISIONS OF SWAP AGREEMENTS

Because of the potentially large exposure which may exist over the term of a swap, each party has an interest in the continued ability of the other party to perform. Accordingly, if the credit-worthiness of one party declines or if legal impediments to its performance arise, the other party may wish to close out the agreement, make alternate arrangements and fix its claim against the first party for its losses, if any, in doing so.

Credit events of acceleration

The events of acceleration or termination of the typical swap agreement usually include a condensed version of the events of default common to loan agreements and apply to both parties: non-payment of amounts under the agreement, breach of a material warranty, breach of a material covenant and insolvency. In addition, in a swap between a corporate counterparty and a bank intermediary, certain clauses, such as the insolvency and cross-default clauses, may be applicable only to the corporate counterparty. Typical default provisions would commence as shown on p. 101.

In the balance of this chapter a party as to which an event of default has occurred is referred to as the 'defaulting party', even though it may not have actually breached its obligations under the agreement.

Supervening illegality

In addition, there would usually be an event of acceleration, though usually not termed an event of default, for occurrences such as supervening illegality and imposition of withholding taxes which change the legal and regulatory assumptions held by the parties when entering the agreement. This acceleration event roughly parallels the change in law provision in Eurodollar loan agreements requiring prepayments in the event of illegality or permitting prepayment in the event of the imposition of withholding taxes. Often agreements between parties in a single jurisdiction (eg, two US entities) do not have illegality provisions. Even if between two US entities, however, many regulatory institutions in the US, such as banks, require such provisions on the theory that regulatory agencies may at some future date hold those activities to be inappropriate. For instance, the US Comptroller of the Currency has reportedly been considering whether or not the quantity of swaps written by US national banks should be limited or

ARTICLE V
TERMINATION

Section 5.01. Notice of Accelerated Settlement Date. Either party may, by notice to the other (effective no earlier than five Business Days after being given and specifying in reasonable detail the basis therefor), designate as the Accelerated Settlement Date a Business Day which is within thirty Business Days after:

(*a*) *Events of Default.* A day on which any of the following Events of Default shall have occurred and be continuing with respect to the other:

(i) *Default in Exchange.* Default on any Settlement Date by a party in payment of any amount under Section 2.01 and continuance of such default for .... Business Days; or

(ii) *Representation or Warranty.* Any representation or warranty made by a party herein is untrue in any material respect, or any schedule, report, notice, certificate or writing furnished by a party to the other hereunder is untrue in any material respect on the date as of which the facts set forth are stated or certified; or

(iii) *Other Default.* Default in the performance of a party's material agreements herein set forth (and not constituting an Event of Default under the preceding subsection) and continuance of such default for 30 days after notice thereof to such party from the other party; or

(iv) *Insolvency.* [Solely with respect to the Company, the Company] [A party] becomes insolvent or generally does not pay its debts as they become due or admits in writing its inability to pay its debts generally as they become due or is adjudicated a bankrupt or insolvent; or [the Company] [a party] applies for, consents to, or acquieses in the appointment of, a trustee, custodian or receiver for itself or any property thereof, or makes a general assignment for the benefit of creditors; or, in the absence of such application, consent or acquiescence, a trustee, custodian or receiver is appointed for [the Company] [a party] or for a substantial part of its property and is not discharged within 30 days; or [the Company] [a party] winds up its affairs; or any bankruptcy, reorganization, debt arrangement, or other proceedings or case under any bankruptcy or insolvency law, or any dissolution or liquidation proceeding is instituted by (in respect of itself) or against [the Company] [a party] or any material event equivalent to any of the foregoing shall occur under the laws of any jurisdiction, and if instituted against [the Company] [a party] is consented to or acquiesced in by it or remains for 60 days undismissed; or [the Company] [a party] takes any corporate action to authorize any of the actions described in this Section 5.01(*a*)(ii); or

(v) *Cross Default.* [Solely with respect to the Company, the Company] [A party] shall default in the payment when due (whether at maturity, by acceleration or otherwise) of any obligation for money borrowed or guaranteed or default in the performance of, or there shall occur any other event of default under, any agreement under which any such obligation is created, if the effect of such default or event of default is to cause such obligation to become, or to permit the holder or holders of such obligation (or a trustee on behalf of such holder or holders) to declare such obligation, due prior to its expressed maturity; [or]

[(vi) *Cessation of Banking Business.* Solely with respect to the Bank, the Bank shall cease to conduct a general banking business;]

whether or not 'speculative' swaps are permissible to national banks. It is, of course, unlikely that any change in law would be retroactive. Nonetheless, at least in an international context, many parties still require that an additional clause be added to the foregoing acceleration section (after Section 5.03(a)) as follows:

> or
>
>   (*b*)   *Illegality or Taxes.*   Any change in applicable laws or regulations or in the interpretation thereof by any governmental or regulatory entity charged with the administration thereof shall have made it unlawful for either party to continue to perform its material obligations under this Agreement or shall have resulted in the party giving such notice becoming obligated to pay the other party material amounts under Section 3.04 in respect of Taxes.

Requirements for payments on termination may, of course, not be enforceable if a change in law has prohibited performance under the swap agreement. However, including an illegality event as an acceleration event does serve several purposes. First, the illegality may be prospective, and the early close-out permits the parties to make the relevant payments before the illegality arises, thereby preserving the economic benefit of the transaction. Second, if there is a netting out on closing in a currency swap, the parties might well be permitted to make the close-out payments in one currency although a party is no longer permitted to pay or receive the other currency.

A related, but independent, provision in the agreement may state that the obligations of the parties are not discharged by reason of supervening illegality applicable to one or both of the parties. Without this type of provision, the party for whom it has become illegal to perform could claim under general principles of contract law that its obligations under the agreement had been discharged by reason of the illegality and that it had no further liability thereunder, not even for damages incurred by the other party. Generally, however, parties are permitted to agree between themselves as to allocation of the risk of illegality. This is not likely to be enforceable by specific performance (ie, compelling a party to perform an illegal act), but the intent of the express provision is to preserve the rights of each party to damages, as a matter of contract law, in the event that the other party does not perform and claims illegality as a discharge. Of course, if the illegality is of such a nature that it prohibits any payments from one party to the other, even the claim for damages would probably not be enforceable. This provision therefore supplements the acceleration event for illegality: it may preserve the right to damages in the event that the illegality prevents certain payments at close-out; and it may preserve for each party the right to damages in respect of interim payments without forcing it to terminate the entire agreement. Such a provision would be as shown on p. 103.

Termination and close-out payments

Probably the single most interesting, complicated and variable aspect of swap documentation is the manner in which the parties treat the effects of acceleration. Virtually all agreements provide for termination of the future

> **Section 5.02. Supervening Illegality.** Without prejudice to Section 5.01(*b*), a party shall not be excused from performance hereunder by supervening illegality (whether by reason of passage or promulgation of a new law, regulation or interpretation or of failure to obtain any required governmental consent or approval), impossibility or frustration, *provided,* that no party shall be obligated to violate any applicable law by reason of this Section, but each party shall retain its right to damages hereunder in the event that the other party does not perform because of supervening illegality, impossibility or frustration.

rights and obligations of the parties on acceleration. Further, almost all agreements contain one of the following three types of additional close-out provisions to provide compensation for early termination: a general indemnity by a defaulting party to the non-defaulting party; a requirement that the defaulting party pay to the other party an amount, if any, calculated in accordance with a formula or other mechanism for quantifying redeployment gains and losses, with the non-defaulting party not making a payment under any circumstances; and a requirement that, based on a calculation under a formula, one party or the other pays an amount regardless of default (although default enters into certain elements of the formula). None of these provisions is without legal risk, although some are subject to more defences than others.

Gain or loss on termination

The position of the Bank and the Company in our example can be illustrated as follows:

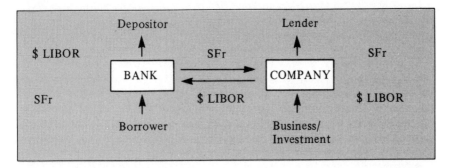

As discussed above in Chapter 6, termination of a swap agreement will leave the parties with unmatched revenues and liabilities. At least one party may seek compensation from the other for its losses in making alternative arrangements to match those revenues and liabilities. Due to the movement of rates and market conditions, creating alternative arrangements on terms similar to the now terminated swap will most probably result in a gain to one party and a loss to the other.

For example, if the Bank and the Company in our example wish to quantify the amount of the gain or loss on an early termination based on then current rates, how would they do it? Until recently, the almost universally accepted method of calculating gains or losses was by reference to a series of borrowings and investments. The Bank needs to receive a stream of dollar LIBOR interest payments on the scheduled settlement dates plus the notional dollar principal amount on the final settlement date. It therefore might put on deposit in the London interbank market an amount equal to the notional dollar principal amount for the remainder of the period, thereby receiving semi-annual dollar LIBOR payments and the notional dollar principal amount at maturity. It further needs to create a Swiss franc liability on each of the subsequent scheduled settlement dates equal to the fixed rate Swiss franc amount it was to pay then, including, in the case of the final settlement date, the notional Swiss franc principal amount. It therefore might borrow Swiss francs in an amount and at a fixed rate sufficient to recreate that flow of payments.

The Company requires the reverse. It might borrow an amount equal to the notional dollar principal amount in the London interbank market, thereby recreating a liability for interest at LIBOR on each settlement date and a liability for the notional principal dollar amount on the final settlement date. It then might invest in Swiss francs in an amount and at a fixed rate sufficient to recreate its right to receive the agreed amount of Swiss francs on each settlement date.

Following these borrowings and investments, the position of the parties is as follows.

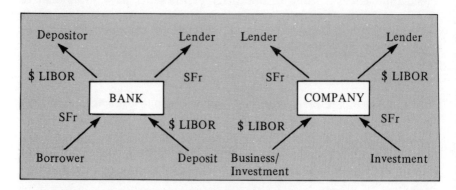

Since the funds which each party invests will be derived from converting the funds which it borrows, the difference (at the spot exchange rates on the close-out date) between the amount of Swiss francs required to be so borrowed/invested on the close-out date and the notional dollar principal amount thus represents the basic gain or loss to the respective parties on the termination date.

Alternatively, and in a recent development, the parties may look to the cost or profit in writing a replacement swap for that being terminated.

Description of indemnity and formula

In an indemnity-oriented agreement, the agreement typically will provide that the future obligations are terminated and the party deemed in default will indemnify the other for its damages. If the close-out is a neutral one (illegality or taxes), sometimes the parties indemnify each other, splitting the difference, and sometimes the party closing out is treated as if it were in default and is obligated to indemnify the other party. Despite this apparent simplicity, there is a recent tendency to expand the indemnity by referring to different steps which the parties may take to mitigate their future contingent losses.

A typical approach based on an indemnity which would be applicable to both currency and interest swaps is as follows.

> **Section 5.03. Termination and Indemnity.** On the Accelerated Settlement Date, the obligations of the parties under Section 2.01 shall terminate forthwith. Upon such termination, the party receiving a notice under Section 5.01 [by reason of an Event of Default with respect to it] ('the defaulting party') shall be liable on demand by the party giving such notice ('the non-defaulting party') to reimburse the non-defaulting party for the amount of any loss suffered or costs or expenses incurred by the non-defaulting party as a consequence of such termination. For the purposes of this Section 5.03, each party expressly acknowledges that the other party is, or may become, a party to one of more agreements or may enter into one or more arrangements, providing for one or more transactions which are the reverse of the transactions contained herein and which cannot be terminated if this Agreement is terminated [following an Event of Default] and to which agreement or agreements or arrangement or arrangements the non-defaulting party shall be entitled to refer for the purpose of computing its losses, costs and expenses.

Close-out provisions in a currency swap agreement using a formula traditionally compare two closing amounts based on a series of borrowings and investments as set forth above: the Bank would pay to the Company the Swiss franc closing amount which, as will be noticed above, is the present value of the future Swiss franc payments (which includes a principal component at maturity); and the Company would pay to the Bank the notional dollar principal amount. Each party implicitly is borrowing the amount it pays and investing the amount it receives. Under some agreements, each party pays its closing amount to the other or whichever party has the larger closing amount (at then spot rates) pays the difference. Under other agreements, the defaulting party is required to pay the excess of its closing amount over the other closing amount but the non-defaulting party is not required to pay if its closing amount is the larger. In addition to formula calculations, the defaulting party is usually obligated to pay enforcement and other directly related costs.

The element of fault becomes relevant in the formulas in the choice of the rates used in discounting the relevant fixed-rate amounts back to the close-out date. Referring again to the termination example above, the Company can presumably invest the Swiss francs in a high quality obligation at a lower rate than that at which the Bank can borrow Swiss francs. Thus, depending on whether or not the formula uses the lower investment rate or the higher borrowing rate as the discount factor, the Swiss franc closing amount is larger or smaller. Choice of the investment rate or the borrowing rate generally depends upon which of the parties is perceived to be at fault. Thus, if the Bank is in default, the investment rate would be used and, if the Company is in default the Bank's borrowing rate would be used. Often, if the close-out event is 'neutral', such as illegality or imposition of withholding taxes, the parties will agree to use as the discount rate an average of the borrowing and investment rates. The discount rate can be either a separate rate for each future settlement date or a single rate based on redeployment of the Swiss franc notional principal amount for the full term. In addition, some banks will include in the discount rates, or in other ways, compensation for any applicable reserve costs or for balance sheet utilisation. Additional adjustments can also be made if the swap involved margins

[Currency Swap]

Section 5.03.   Exchange on Accelerated Settlement Date.   On the Second Business Day before the Accelerated Settlement Date, the Reference Bank shall determine the Dollar Closing Amount and the Swiss Franc Closing Amount.   On the Accelerated Settlement Date, subject to the terms and conditions contained in this Agreement, the Company agrees to pay to the Bank the Dollar Closing Amount and the Bank agrees to pay to the Company the Swiss Franc Closing Amount, each such payment to be in consideration of the other, *provided* that each party shall be entitled to deduct from the amount payable by it under this Section all amounts, if any, due to it under Sections 2.01, 5.04, 5.05 and 6.03 as of the Accelerated Settlement Date. As of the Accelerated Settlement Date, the rights and obligations of the parties under Section 2.01 with respect to Settlement Dates falling after the Accelerated Settlement Date shall be terminated and discharged in full. The parties agree that the amounts recoverable pursuant to this Section are the reasonable pre-estimates of loss likely to be sustained by the parties as a result of an early termination and are not a penalty, and that (if the Accelerated Settlement Date is designated by reason of an Event of Default) such amounts are payable as liquidated damages or (if the Accelerated Settlement Date is designated by reason of a change in laws) such amounts are payable to preserve the economic benefits of the transaction.

[Definitions: From definition section or schedule]

Dollar Closing Amount means (i) if the Accelerated Settlement Date is a Settlement Date, the Dollar Principal Amount or (ii) if the Accelerated Settlement Date is not a Settlement Date, the Present Value of the sum of the Dollar Amount scheduled to be paid on the next following Settlement Date plus, if such next following scheduled Settlement Date is not the last scheduled Settlement Date, the Dollar Principal Amount, discounted from such next scheduled Settlement Date using a discount rate equal to LIBOR for the period between such two dates;

Swiss Franc Closing Amount means the aggregate of the Present Values of all Swiss Franc Amounts then scheduled for each Settlement Date falling after the Accelerated Settlement Date, in each case discounted from its originally scheduled Settlement Date using a discount factor equal to:

(i)   if the Accelerated Settlement Date shall have been established by the Company by reason of an Event of Default with respect to the Bank, the average, determined by the Reference Bank, of the yields to maturity for investments selected by the Reference Bank in a principal amount approximately equal to [the relevant Swiss Franc Amount] [the Swiss Franc Principal Amount], denominated in Swiss Francs and issued by [insert agreed description of high-quality Swiss franc bonds] trading in a reasonable volume in the secondary market with maturities as near as practicable to [such originally scheduled Settlement Date] [the Termination Date] (such yields to maturity to be determined from the closing prices of such securities as quoted in the daily official bond quotation of the relevant stock exchange or, if not available, other reputable reporting source), *provided* that, if there are no such [specify type of bonds] available, the Reference Bank shall use investments issued by the most substantial and creditworthy entities, in its good faith opinion, available;

and

(ii) if the Accelerated Settlement Date shall have been established by the Bank by reason of an Event of Default with respect to the Company, the estimated cost, expressed as an interest rate per annum, determined by the Reference Bank as either, at the option of the Bank,

(A) the interest rate per annum the Bank would have to pay on a fixed rate and annual payment basis for borrowing the relevant amount from the Accelerated Settlement Date to [such originally scheduled Settlement Date] [the Termination Date] or

(B) the notional interest rate per annum applicable to the obligation of the Bank to deliver amounts corresponding to those hereunder on the due dates required hereunder pursuant to a currency exchange agreement with a substantial and creditworthy third party;

and

(iii) If the Accelerated Settlement Date shall have been established under circumstances other than those set forth in clause (i) and (ii), the average of the discount rates determined in accordance with clause (i) and (ii), respectively.*

over or below LIBOR. A weakness of this approach is the use of top credit government securities for redeployment on the investment side, since the relevant party has replaced a corporate risk with a government risk. This defect can be avoided by providing for investments in securities with public ratings comparable to those of the counterparty on the date of entering the agreement.

If the closing date is not a settlement date no adjustment is required in calculating the Swiss franc closing amount for amounts not yet payable but accrued as of the early termination date. The formula implicitly allows for this in taking the present value of the next scheduled Swiss franc payment which includes such accrued amounts. However, the dollar closing amount must be adjusted to take into consideration dollar interest accrued and redeployment gain or loss in the current interest period. This is most easily handled by calculating the dollar closing amount as the present value of the notional principal amount plus the variable dollar payment scheduled for the next settlement date, using a discount factor of LIBOR for the interim period. Such a calculation brings into account (a) the amount accrued through the early termination date, (b) gains or losses on redeployment for the balance of the current variable period and (c) the fact that payment is being made prior to the date scheduled.

A typical, traditional currency swap approach based on mutual and actual payments calculated by an investment/borrowing formula would be as shown on p. 106 and above.

The more recent 'replacement' approach derives from the large volume of swaps which are currently being written and the number of active swap participants. It is based on the cost of writing a replacement swap. Thus, if the Company were in default, the closing amount payable to (or by) the Bank would be the cost (or profit) to the Bank in inducing a substantial

* This definition treats a neutral close-out event, such as illegality or taxes, as neutral to the parties.

[Currency Swap]

Section 5.03. Accelerated Settlement Date Payments.   On the second Business Day before the Accelerated Settlement Date, the Reference Bank shall determine the Termination Value.   On the Accelerated Settlement Date: if the Termination Value is a positive amount, the Company agrees [,unless the Accelerated Settlement Date shall have been designated by the Company by reason of an Event of Default with respect to the Bank,] to pay the Termination Value to the Bank; if the Termination Value is a negative amount, the Bank agrees [,unless the Accelerated Settlement Date shall have been designated by the Bank by reason of an Event of Default with respect to the Company,] to pay the absolute value of the Termination Value to the Company; and if, as so determined,the Termination Value is zero [or if the party otherwise required to pay the excess amount is excused from payment because the Accelerated Settlement Date was designated by reason of an Event of Default with respect to the other party], the parties will be deemed to have performed their relevant obligations on the Accelerated Settlement Date for purposes of this Section 5.03 without any payment having to be made. As of the Accelerated Settlement Date, the rights and obligations of the parties under Section 2.01 with respect to Settlement Dates falling after the Accelerated Settlement Date and with respect to all other amounts then due and owing as of the Accelerated Settlement Date (other than under this Section 5.03) shall be terminated and discharged in full. The parties agree that the amounts, if any, recoverable pursuant to this Section 5.03 are the reasonable pre-estimates of loss likely to be sustained by the parties as a result of an early termination and are not a penalty, and that (if the Accelerated Settlement Date is designated by reason of an Event of Default) such amounts are payable as liquidated damages or (if the Accelerated Settlement Date is designated by reason of a change in laws) such amounts are payable to preserve the economic benefits of the transaction. In calculating the Termination Value,

[Definitions; From definition section or schedule]

  Dollar Closing Amount   [same as above];

  Dollar Equivalent   means, with respect to an amount of Swiss Francs, the amount in Dollars which the Bank could buy with, and the Company could sell for, such amount of Swiss Francs at the Reference Bank's [mid-] spot rate of exchange as of two Business Days prior to the Accelerated Settlement Date for the [purchase] [and] [sale] of Swiss Francs [with] [and] [for] Dollars in London or New York City, after taking into consideration all customary charges, costs, premiums and other expenses in connection with such [purchase] [and] [sale];

  Present Value   [same as above];

  [*Reference Dealers* means ...., ... and ...., or such other entities as the parties shall agree;]

  Replacement Value means the amount in Dollars (which may be negative) equal to (a) the arithmetic mean, determined by the Reference Bank as of 11:00 a.m. (London time) on the day two Business Days prior to the Accelerated Settlement Date, of the amounts which are quoted by each of [three leading commercial banks in ....selected in good faith by the Reference Bank] [the Reference Dealers] as the respective all-in fees (including documentation costs) which they would charge, or would be willing to pay,

       (i) the Bank, if the Accelerated Settlement Date shall have been established by the Bank by reason of an Event of Default with respect to the Company, or

       (ii) the Company, if the Accelerated Settlement Date shall have been established by the Company by reason of an Event of Default with respect to the Bank,

to enter into an agreement, effective as of the Accelerated Settlement Date and providing for such [bank] [Reference Dealer] to obtain and incur substantially the same rights and obligations with respect to the Bank or the Company, as the case may be, as the rights and obligations of the Company or the Bank, respectively, set forth herein falling after the Accelerated Settlement Date (without regard to the termination of such rights and obligations in Section 5.03), or (b) if the Accelerated Settlement Date shall have been established under circumstances other than set forth in clause (a), the average of amounts determined in accordance with subclause (i) and (ii) of clause (a), *provided*, that if the Reference Bank, after reasonable efforts, is unable to obtain quotations of such fees from all [such banks] [Reference Dealers], 'Replacement Value' shall be determined on the basis of quotations of such fee or fees obtained from one or two [such banks] [Reference Dealers]; and *further provided*, that if any [such bank] [Reference Deaier] states that it would require such a fee from the Bank or would be willing to pay such a fee to the Company, such quoted amount shall be a positive number and, if any [such bank] [Reference Dealer] states that it would require such a fee from the Company or would be willing to pay such a fee to the Bank, such quoted amount shall be a negative number, and the aforesaid calculations shall be made accordingly;

Termination Value means the amount in Dollars (which may be negative) equal to the aggregate of (a) the Replacement Value or, if the Reference Bank was unable after reasonable efforts to determine the Replacement Value, the remainder of the Dollar Closing Amount minus the Dollar Equivalent of the Swiss Franc Closing Amount, plus (b) all amounts then due and owing by the Company to the Bank under this Agreement (other than under Section 5.03), minus (c) all amounts then due and owing by the Bank to the Company under this Agreement (other then under Section 5.03);

Swiss Franc Closing Amount [same as above];

and creditworthy third party to enter into a swap with the Bank on substantially the same terms as those set forth in the agreement being terminated. If the Bank were in default, the relevant closing amounts would be those which the Company would have to pay to, or would be able to receive from, such a party to write the replacement swap. If the event of acceleration were a neutral event, the parties could choose to average the two rates out. Such a cost could be determined on the basis of quotations from either a list of specified swap participants or entities which are described generally. A weakness of this approach also is that it does not account for the difference between the creditworthiness of the replacement swap party and the original party. In addition, it contains an implicit assumption that the swap market will continue for the term of the agreement (which may be ten or more years) at its current or increased levels. While this may be likely, it is not as certain as is the likelihood of the continued availability of a market for borrowing and investing. The replacement approach could, however, also be utilised with the borrowing/investment approach providing a fallback position on a netted basis, as shown on pp. 108–109.

In interest swaps in the same currency, the parties generally provide for netted closing payments as follows.

[Interest Swap]

Section 5.03.   Accelerated Settlement Date Payments.   On the second Business Day before the Accelerated Settlement Date, the Reference Bank shall determine the difference between the Fixed Closing Amount and the Variable Closing Amount. If, as so determined, the Fixed Closing Amount is greater than the Variable Closing Amount, the Bank on the Accelerated Settlement Date shall [, unless the Accelerated Settlement Date shall have been designated by the Bank by reason of an Event of Default with respect to the Company,] pay the difference to the Company; if, as so determined, the Variable Closing Amount is greater than the Fixed Closing Amount, the Company on the Accelerated Settlement Date shall [, unless the Accelerated Settlement Date shall have been designated by the Company by reason of an Event of Default with respect to the Bank,] pay the difference to the Bank; and if, as so determined, there is no such difference [or the party otherwise required to pay the excess amount is excused from payment because of the Accelerated Settlement Date was designated by reason of an Event of Default with respect to the other party], the parties will be deemed to have performed their relevant obligations on the Accelerated Settlement Date for purposes of this Section 5.03 without any payment having to be made. As of the Accelerated Settlement Date, the rights and obligations of the parties under Section 2.01 with respect to Settlement Dates falling after the Accelerated Settlement Date and with respect to all other amounts then due and owing as of the Accelerated Date (other than under this Section 5.03) shall be terminated and discharged in full. The parties agree that the amounts, if any, recoverable pursuant to this Section 5.03 are the reasonable pre-estimates of loss likely to be sustained by the parties as a result of an early termination and are not a penalty, and that (if the Accelerated Settlement Date is designated by reason of an Event of Default) such amounts are payable as liquidated damages or (if the Accelerated Settlement Date is designated by reason of a change in laws) such amounts are payable to preserve the economic benefits of the transaction.

However, in determining the respective closing amounts, two different close-out approaches based on borrowings and investments are often used. The first method (Approach A) is similar to that described above for cross-currency interest swaps, which compares (a) the aggregate present values of each fixed rate payment from its due date and of the notional principal amount from the final settlement date, as the fixed closing amount, with (b) the notional principal amount, as the variable closing amount. Again, the discount rate can be either a separate rate for each future settlement date or a single rate based on redeployment of the notional principal amount for the full term. Accrued amounts and redeployment gains or losses on variable payments resulting from close-out other than on a settlement date are implicitly covered as in the currency swap provisions set forth above.

The second method (Approach B) disregards notional payments of principal at maturity (since principal payments are equal in amount and there is no currency risk) and determines damages only on the basis of the change in the fixed rate. The parties compare only the fixed redeployment rate at the time of close-out for the notional principal amount over the remaining period of the transaction and the original fixed rate. The product of the difference between those rates, expressed as a percentage, times the notional principal amount is then discounted back from each settlement date to the close-out date. The discount rate can be either the redeployment rate (eg, the borrowing or investment rate, as the case may be) or the lower investment rate in all cases. The latter is often used in situations where the non-defaulting party never pays to the defaulting party since use of the lower rate maximises the present value of the redeployment differential and therefore would tend to be more onerous on a defaulting party. In Approach B, however, a separate calculation must then be made to provide for payment of accrued amounts and calculation of any gain or loss on redeployment during the current variable period resulting from close-out other than on a settlement date.

In both approaches, the element of fault is reflected in the choice of redeployment rate: a lower investment rate (eg, a treasury note rate) or a higher borrowing rate. If the single, long-term redeployment rate is used in Approach A and the same redeployment rate is used as the discount factor in Approach B, the same numbers will result (except for treatment of close-out other than on a settlement date). The advantages of Approach A are that the provisions are shorter and handle several different complexities (accrued amounts and variable redeployment gains or losses) implicitly but accurately. The advantage of Approach B is that, by focusing on the difference between the agreed fixed rate and the redeployment rate, it is conceptually easier to explain the rationale behind it to a counterparty. This often is the case despite the greater length of Approach B and the fact that the end result may be the same under both Approaches. (See pp. 112–114).

Of course, the 'replacement' swap approach could also be combined with Approach A or B as for currency swaps above.

Other factors may marginally affect the efficacy of the foregoing arrangements in fully covering the parties (balance sheet utilisation costs, lack of access to a currency, opportunity costs, gearing restraints and inability to borrow at LIBOR), and can be provided for in the formulas if the parties desire.

Indemnity and formula compared

The usual arguments in favour of a general indemnity by the defaulting party rather than payment under a formula are: simplicity in drafting; the difficulty in understanding the formulas which would otherwise be used; and lack of consensus as to what is an adequate close-out formula. The indemnity is the simplest to draft, although it often results in complications as to how to handle an early closing as a result of 'neutral' events such as illegality or imposition of taxes. In addition, there is a recent tendency in indemnity-oriented agreements to expand on permissible close-out steps, so that the indemnity begins to look very much like a formula. Objections based on the complexity of the formulas beg the question since in proving damages under an indemnity a party would in any event have to convince a court that it has incurred damages, using an analysis similar to that set

[Interest Swap]

[Definitions: from definition section or schedule]

[Common to both Approach A and Approach B]

Present Value means, with respect to a given amount and date, the value, determined two Business Days prior to the Accelerated Settlement Date, of such amount discounted on [an annual] [a semi-annual] payment basis from such date to the Accelerated Settlement Date;

Redeployment Rate means:

(i)   if the Accelerated Settlement Date shall have been established by the Company by reason of an Event of Default with respect to the Bank and there shall not then have occurred and be continuing an Event of Default with respect to the Company, the Treasury Rate;

or

(ii)   if the Accelerated Settlement Date shall have been established under circumstances other than those set forth in clause (i), the estimated cost, expressed as an interest rate per annum, determined by the Reference Bank as either, at the option of the Bank,

(A)   the interest rate per annum the Bank would have to pay on a fixed rate and annual payment basis for borrowing the [relevant amount] from the Accelerated Settlement Date to the Termination Date or

(B)   the notional interest rate per annum applicable to the obligation of the Bank to deliver amounts corresponding to those hereunder on the due dates hereunder pursuant to an interest exchange agreement with a substantial and creditworthy third party;*

Treasury Rate means the rate determined by the Reference Bank as of the second Business Day prior to the Accelerated Settlement Date to be equal to the [highest] [average] annual yield to maturity which [two leading US government securities dealers of recognised standing, selected by the Reference Bank, estimate] the Reference Bank could have obtained if it had purchased US Treasury notes in a principal amount equal to the Notional Principal Amount with a maturity as close as is possible to the Termination Date and trading in the secondary market in reasonable volume at a price reasonably close to par with payments being made semi-annually, all in accordance with United States domestic practice;

[Approach A]

Fixed Closing Amount means the remainder in Dollars of (i) the sum of (A) the aggregate of the Present Values of the Fixed Amounts then scheduled for Settlement Dates falling after the Accelerated Settlement Date, in each case discounted from its originally scheduled Settlement Date using a discount rate equal to the Redeployment Rate,

---

* This definition treats a neutral close-out event, such as illegality or taxes, as favourable to the Bank on the intermediary theory.

and (B) the Present Value of the Notional Principal Amount from the Termination Date using a discount rate equal to the Redeployment Rate, minus (ii) all amounts then due and owing by the Company to the Bank under this Agreement; and

Variable Closing Amount means the remainder in Dollars of (i) if the Accelerated Settlement Date is a Settlement Date, the Notional Principal Amount or, if the Accelerated Settlement Date is not a Settlement Date, the Present Value of the sum of the Notional Principal Amount and the Variable Amount scheduled to be paid on the next following Settlement Date discounted from such next scheduled Settlement Date using a discount rate equal to LIBOR for the period between such two dates, minus (ii) all amounts then due and owing by the Bank to the Company under this Agreement.

[Approach B]

Accrued Fixed Amount means, if the Accelerated Settlement Date is not a Settlement Date, the product of the Notional Principal Amount, the Fixed Rate* and a fraction the numerator of which is the number of days (adjusted to conform to a year of 360 days and twelve 30-day months) elapsed since the immediately preceding Settlement Date and the denominator of which is 360;

Accrued Variable Amount means, if the Accelerated Settlement Date is not a Settlement Date, the product of the Notional Principal Amount, the Variable Rate in effect for the then current Interest Period and a fraction the numerator of which is the number of days elapsed since the immediately preceding Settlement Date and the denominator of which is 360;

Fixed Closing Amount means the aggregate in Dollars of

(i) the Accrued Fixed Amount;

plus

(ii) if the Redeployment Rate is less than the Fixed Rate, the Redeployment Differential;

plus

(iii) if the Accelerated Settlement Date is not a Settlement Date, the variable redeployment gain, being the Present Value of the excess, if any, of (i) the product of (A) the Notional Principal Amount, (B) LIBOR for the period from the Accelerated Settlement Date to the next following Settlement Date and (C) a fraction the numerator of which is the number of days in such period and the denominator of which is 360 over (ii) the remainder of (A) the Variable Amount scheduled to be paid on such next following Settlement Date minus (B) the Accrued Variable Amount, such excess being discounted from such next following Settlement Date using a discount factor equal to such LIBOR;

minus

(iv) all amounts then due and owing by the Company to the Bank under this Agreement.

* Being the rate used in calculating the Fixed Amount.

Redeployment Differential means the sum of the Present Values of separate amounts calculated for each of the Settlement Dates falling after the Accelerated Settlement Date, each of which separate amounts (i) is equal to the product of (A) the Notional Principal Amount, (B) the difference between the Redeployment Rate and the Fixed Rate, (C) one-half**, and (D) if the Accelerated Settlement Date is not a Settlement Date and in respect of the amount calculated for the next following Settlement Date only, a fraction the numerator of which is the number of days (adjusted to conform to a year of 360 days and twelve 30-day months) remaining until such next following Settlement Date and the denominator of which is 360 and (ii) is discounted from the relevant Settlement Date using a discount factor equal to the Treasury Rate.

Variable Closing Amount means the aggregate in Dollars of

(i) the Accrued Variable Amount;

plus

(ii) if the Redeployment Rate is greater than the Fixed Rate, the Redeployment Differential;

plus

(iii) if the Accelerated Settlement Date is not a Settlement Date, the variable redeployment loss, being the Present Value of the excess, if any, of (i) the remainder of (A) the Variable Amount scheduled to be paid on the next following Settlement Date minus (B) the Accrued Variable Amount over (ii) the product of (A) the Notional Principal Amount, (B) LIBOR for the period from the Accelerated Settlement Date to such next following Settlement Date and (C) a fraction the numerator of which is the number of days in such period and the denominator of which is 360, such excess being discounted from such next following Settlement Date using a discount factor equal to such LIBOR;

minus

(iv) all amounts then due and owing by the Bank to the Company under this Agreement.

forth in the formulas although now with the other side arguing against the reasonableness of the claim. Further, in our experience, the parties have invariably been able to agree a formula which takes into consideration different investment and borrowing rates.

In addition, a general indemnity lends less certainty to the agreement. Even if the right to be indemnified is not subject to defence, the amount claimable under the indemnity (since not specified) is. An indemnity is generally strictly construed against the indemnified party, ie, when there is ambiguity or doubt, the benefit thereof accrues to the party giving the indemnity. It may not be enforced with respect to contingent losses, and the burden of proof is on the indemnified party to show its actual losses. Finally, an indemnity is subject to defences such as failure to mitigate or avoid loss. While these may be desirable in principle, the effect in application is to raise potential defences to an indemnity claim, based both on questions of fact and law, which the indemnified party must overcome prior

** Assumes semi-annual fixed payments.

to recovery and which will not be summarily disposed of at the early stages of litigation. On the other hand, an indemnity, while difficult to enforce by the indemnified party, may result in an even larger claim than the parties would have anticipated if the indemnified party claims consequential damages or damages based on circumstances which, while not known to the indemnitor, should or could have been known by it. Enforcement thus becomes less certain from both parties' standpoint.

The formula approach (whether based on borrowing and investment or replacement), since it rests on an expressly agreed contractual provision, is subject to fewer such defences and uncertainties. A theoretical risk exists that provisions based on the formula approach would not be upheld if found to result in a 'grossly disproportionate' or 'unconscionable' recovery not related to actual damage. Parties attempt to limit this risk by characterising the payments as liquidated damages. While helpful, such a characterisation might not be technically correct and, if the results are found to be 'grossly disproportionate', such characterisation will not in any event stop a court from characterising the payments as a penalty or contrary to public policy, and therefore not enforceable. However, since the formulas are invariably based on actual market redeployment rates at the time of close-out and on redeployment steps generally regarded as reasonable, it would be highly unlikely for a characterization such as 'grossly disproportionate' or 'unconscionable' to apply.

The formula thus lends a greater certainty to both parties than does a general indemnity. While more complicated to draft, formulas are not difficult to work through and can be calculated either by the non-defaulting party or a third party reference bank. Since it is primarily a calculation exercise, the claim is more likely to be disposed of early rather than late in the litigation process. Also, each party is able to refer to the agreement and determine its exposure at any time. While subject to certain theoretical defences, the formula approach, based as it is on reasonable expectations at the time the agreement is entered, is more likely to be upheld and thus to fulfil the parties' expectations than a general indemnity based on a variety of contingent expectations which are subject to different interpretations.

One-sided payments and mutual payments compared

Another legal risk, using either the formula or indemnity approach, results from the close-out payment only being required to be made by the defaulting party. The advantage of the one way close out appears to be the concern that a payment to the defaulting party could be regarded as an incentive for it to breach and to close out an agreement no longer regarded as desirable. This is unjustified for several reasons. First, if one party were to seek to avoid an agreement by breaching it and thereby hoping to receive a close-out payment, it is not necessarily able to do so. If it fails to make a payment, the other party need not close out. It can simply sue the defaulting party for that amount, together with interest at the default rate and lawyers' fees. This may pose some difficulties for the non-defaulting party, but far more difficulties for the defaulting party which has no valid defence. Second, the rates that are used in the formula will not fully protect the defaulting party and it will incur some loss. Third, it is likely, though not always certain, that if application of a formula would show an amount owing to the defaulter, scheduled payments otherwise owing to the defaulter would be greater than those owing by it. Thus, since payments are conditional against each other, at that point in time, the non-defaulting party should generally be able to provide for its receipts out of the cancellation or deferral of its payments. Fourth, turning the argument in favour of a one-sided payment around, such a structure may be an incentive to a party to take advantage of a technical default to terminate the agreement. Thus, if one party is in a 'loss' position in the swap and the second party commits a technical default, the first party may seize the opportunity to terminate the agreement rather than to respond to attempts to cure the technical default. The real reason for the one-sided payment provision is based on the parties' visceral reaction against a non-defaulting party having to pay anything to a defaulting party, even though such payment still leaves the non-defaulting party whole.

The result of the one-sided indemnity/formula is that the non-defaulting party may be able to reap a substantial windfall profit by termination if rates have moved against its position in the swap to the detriment of the defaulting party. There may thus be a higher likelihood of it being deemed a penalty, a forfeiture or against public policy, and therefore not enforceable, than in the case of a payment provision based on actual economic gains and losses of both parties. This 'penalty' aspect of the close-out provision could have uncertain results, which could include the whole provision being held unenforceable. In addition, courts often refuse to uphold termination of agreements by reason of breaches deemed by the court to be immaterial or not central to the performance by the defaulting party of its primary obligations. It would follow that the more onerous the result of termination, the less likely a court would be to view a given breach as central to the agreement. The draconian result of a one-sided payment on close out thus may result either in a court not supporting the agreed close-out payment provisions or not permitting termination on grounds of contract law.

Bankruptcy and insolvency law

A more serious risk, however, arises under the insolvency laws of certain jurisdictions. These laws are applicable to bankruptcy proceedings in the relevant jurisdiction regardless of the choice of contract law, since insolvency principles override the choice of contract law. On the other hand, selecting a jurisdiction's law to govern a contract does not mean that the insolvency laws of that jurisdiction will apply to the contract. The types of laws which present the most difficulties are reorganisation-oriented insolvency laws. The principle behind these laws is that the courts stay enforcement of creditors' rights so that the debtor will be able to readjust its affairs and emerge as a viable entity. The insolvency laws of, eg, the US and France are reorganisation-oriented. The laws of England, at the moment, are liquidation-oriented, which is to say that in insolvency proceedings the thrust is on distributing assets rather than facilitating a reorganisation. The discussion in this section is thus less applicable to a swap agreement in which an English company is party than to a swap agreement with a company incorporated in the US (or in another reorganisation-oriented jurisdiction) or a company with operations in the US such that it may be subject to US bankruptcy laws.

Let us assume that a party to a swap agreement files a petition for a chapter 11 reorganisation proceeding in the US. We will call it the insolvent party and the other party the solvent party. Let us also assume that, due to movement of rates, the swap agreement is favourable to the insolvent party. That is to say, on a netted basis, payments to it would exceed payments by it. Worded another way, the insolvent party has a profit or equity in the continuance of the agreement.

A swap agreement, where both parties are obligated to perform in the future, is an executory contract. This has important ramifications regarding the ability to terminate the agreement.

The immediate effect of the filing is that there is an automatic stay on the ability to terminate the executory contract. At this point, it is important to determine whether or not a swap agreement constitutes a 'financial accommodation' within the meaning of the US Bankruptcy Code. The answer is not clear: a loan is a financial accommodation; agreements to issue a guarantee of payment and a letter of credit are financial accommodations; and a swap may or may not be a financial accommodation. Characterisation of the agreement as a financial accommodation in the recitals, while helpful, is not dispositive.

If a swap agreement is a financial accommodation, the termination provisions would generally be effective. In this case, it may be useful to include in the agreement a provision for an automatic termination if a party files an insolvency petition or takes corporate action to do so. If such a provision is not included, the solvent party would apply to the bankruptcy court to lift the stay. Even if such a provision is included, the solvent party would prudently wish to obtain the court's concurrence that the agreement is a financial accommodation.

If the court determines that a swap is a financial accommodation, the trustee in bankruptcy cannot assume the agreement and the court will allow its termination, in which case the next issue would be the recovery of damages, which is discussed below. However, if a party in interest objects (eg, the trustee in bankruptcy for the insolvent party), the court may permit the termination on modified terms if any equity of the insolvent party would otherwise be lost and the continuance of the agreement is necessary to the successful rehabilitation of the insolvent party.

Since the effect of finding a swap agreement to be a financial accommodation is that the trustee in bankruptcy cannot assume the agreement and thus the agreement terminates, the court may well be influenced in its determination if the insolvent party would lose equity on termination. Therefore, a swap agreement with the right to terminate and a one-way payment structure, where at the time the loss on close out is on the insolvent party, could well result in influencing the court to find that the agreement is not a financial accommodation.

If the court determines that a swap agreement is not a financial accommodation, the trustee in bankruptcy has the right, regardless of an automatic termination provision, any action taken by the solvent party or any non-assignment clause in a swap agreement, either to reject the swap agreement or to assume it and then either to perform it or assign it to a third party.

The desirability of recitals in the agreement may be illustrated here. Interest on unsecured pre-petition debt ceases on filing of the bankruptcy petition. If the swap agreement was entered into by the insolvent party to hedge its interest obligations, the rationale for the swap agreement falls away. If the agreement is explicit as to the intent of the parties, ie, to hedge interest liabilities, the solvent party has a strong argument to the court in favour of lifting the stay and permitting the termination, even if the agreement is held not to be a financial accommodation and the trustee wishes to assume the agreement. Thus, it is important in a swap agreement with a US party, for this among other reasons, to set out the rationale for the parties' purpose in entering the agreement in a few brief recitals.

If the trustee rejects the swap agreement, the next issue is determination of damages, discussed below.

If the trustee assumes or assigns the swap agreement to a third party, the Bankruptcy Code requires the trustee or the new debtor to cure all existing defaults (other, of course, than the event of default occasioned by the bankruptcy filing). It also requires the debtor or assignee to provide 'adequate assurance' of future performance under the contract. In this case, there would have to be a showing of financial ability to perform in the future, which could include collateralisation.

If, due to existing rates, payments are flowing from the solvent party to the insolvent party, it should be relatively easy for the insolvent party to show its ability to make future payments. If the agreement is on a netted basis, the insolvent party can show that amounts are flowing to it and any shift in rates would be unlikely to result in material amounts being payable by it. If payments are made under the swap agreement at different times, the insolvent party can show that it can fund its required payments under the swap agreement through the payments it receives from the solvent party.

Perhaps the court will require some showing that on a movement of rates the insolvent party would be able to perform. In any event, the US bankruptcy court has discretion as to what these assurances are. They are unlikely to be exactly what the solvent party was seeking. Since failure to provide adequate assurances will, in effect, result in termination of the agreement, potential loss of the insolvent party's equity in the agreement on termination could influence the court to approve lesser assurances than it would otherwise be disposed to approve.

If (a) the solvent party has not been permitted to terminate the swap agreement, despite the clear language in the swap agreement, and is required to make several payments under the swap agreement, (b) rates move dramatically and payments are due from the insolvent party, and (c) the insolvent party does not pay, the solvent party would then be able to terminate the agreement and, if not collateralised, to claim damages, as discussed below. The damages determined, however, may in some cases be on a priority basis over other unsecured debt. If the insolvent party is either totally out of funds at this stage or has heavily secured its other debt, this priority may be of little practical benefit.

Thus, the position in which the solvent party can find itself is: its right to terminate is not allowed; it is required to make payments while rates are against it; and, when rates move in favour of the solvent party, the insolvent party ceases to perform and the solvent party has only a prior (but still unsecured) claim.

If the court has approved assignment of the agreement, thereafter the insolvent party is relieved of further liability and the solvent party has recourse solely against the assignee.

If (a) the swap agreement is a financial accommodation and the court has allowed termination, (b) the swap agreement is not a financial accommodation and the trustee has either permitted termination or rejected the agreement, or (c) the trustee assumed the agreement and the debtor subsequently breached the agreement and at that point the solvent party terminated the agreement, the solvent party would file a proof of claim in respect of damages. If the swap agreement contains a two-way formula settlement, it is highly likely that the court would adopt this. If the swap agreement contains a one-way formula, there is a strong possibility that the court would call for testimony and apply its own estimate on the theory that the formula, as it only worked one way, could not be a true measure of damages and would constitute a penalty. If the swap agreement contains an indemnity close-out provision, the court would call for testimony. In addition, the court might have the power to collect 'damages' from the solvent party to the extent of any equity held by the insolvent party. Thus, the two-way formula approach is more likely to survive as the measure of damages than the one-way formula approach or the one-way indemnity. In addition, the solvent party with a one-way close-out exposes itself to liability to the insolvent party on the basis of a court determined estimate of its gain or the insolvent party's lost equity rather than on the basis of the formula.

Summary

The legal problems in termination provisions of swap agreements are reduced by using close-out formulas (including replacement concepts) based on reasonable market calculations which will actually protect to some extent both parties, with a bias in favour of the party contractually agreed to be less at fault. The formula approach seeks to define in advance calculation of the parties' losses or gains on an early termination. The two-way payment approach avoids losses, but also reduces windfalls. Parties to a swap agreement are thus left with a choice between provisions which on their face provide for potentially greater gain to the non-defaulting party but are subject to greater questions of enforceability and provisions which will leave the non-defaulting party only essentially whole but are more likely to be enforced.

Additional termination provisions

Additional provisions may be added which emphasise the conditionality of the cross payments, provide for default interest and permit the parties to close out their positions in the market (in effect 'netting' in one currency) either in respect of one defaulted payment without having to accelerate the entire agreement or in respect of the closing amount on early termination (assuming netting on close out is not otherwise provided). (See pp. 120.)

MISCELLANEOUS PROVISIONS

The miscellaneous provisions are those typically found in loan agreements. The governing law is usually New York or English. Although one can immediately spot stylistic differences between New York law and English law agreements, most swap agreements are enforceable under the laws of either jurisdiction, the only clauses usually which absolutely need to be changed being the governing law clause and the submission to jurisdiction clause. Choice of law, while selecting the law which will govern the contractual terms of the agreement, often does not directly affect whether or not withholding taxes are imposed, the effect of insolvency laws on a party's obligations under the swap agreement, powers of a company to enter into swap agreements or supervening illegality. (See pp. 121–122.)

Section 5.04.*   (a) Termination.   If either party shall fail to tender an amount required to be delivered by it on a Payment Date under Section 2.01 or 5.03** (such party, under such circumstances, herein called the 'Defaulting Party'), the obligations of the party entitled to receive such amount (such party, under such circumstances, herein called the 'Aggrieved Party') to pay the amounts required to be delivered by it on such Payment Date under Section 2.01 or 5.03, as the case may be, shall be suspended until the Defaulting Party tenders such required amount. If such failure continues for .... Business Days, such obligations of the Aggrieved Party shall forthwith terminate but without limiting the Aggrieved Party's rights under the other provisions of this Agreement in respect of the Defaulting Party.

(b)   Damages.   Without limiting the Aggrieved Party's rights under Section 5.01(a) and Section 5.03, the Aggrieved Party shall be entitled to recover from the Defaulting Party:

(i) the amount (if any) by which the net proceeds of the conversion, within the period of ten Business Days after the relevant Payment Date, of (A) the relevant amount of Swiss Francs into Dollars by the Bank (if it is the Aggrieved Party) or (B) the relevant amount of Dollars into Swiss Francs by the Company (if it is the Aggrieved Party), after taking into account all costs and expenses incurred and paid or suffered by the Aggrieved Party in effecting such conversion, falls short of the amount which it was to receive on such Payment Date;

(ii) all costs and expenses (including reasonable attorneys' fees, value added tax, stamp or other similar registration tax or charges and court costs) incurred by the Aggrieved Party in enforcing or preserving its rights under this Agreement; and

(iii) interest under Section 5.05.

(c)   Rights Cumulative.   Except as otherwise expressly set forth herein, the rights (including without limitation the right to establish the Accelerated Settlement Date) and remedies herein provided are cumulative and not exclusive of any rights and remedies provided by law and shall not affect or impair any right to which either party may be entitled by law.

Section 5.05. Default Interest.   Time is of the essence of this Agreement. Without limiting the rights and effects resulting therefrom, if any party shall default in the payment of any amount hereunder when due (without regard to any grace period), it shall pay interest thereon to the party to whom such payment was due on demand (as well after as before judgment) at a rate per annum equal to ....(.... %) above the average, determined on a daily basis by the Reference Bank, of the rates at which overnight call deposits are offered to the Reference Bank in London in such amount and in the currency in which such amount is payable hereunder.

---

* Clauses (a) and (b) would not be necessary in a single currency, interest swap agreement.

** If the close-out provisions in a currency swap agreement provided for either a payment only by the non-defaulting party or a payment on a netted basis in only one currency, the reference in Section 5.04(a) and (b) to Section 5.03 can be eliminated.

ARTICLE VI
MISCELLANEOUS

Section 6.01. Notices. Any notice to be given hereunder shall be given in writing (or by cable or telex addressed to the other party) and shall be deemed to have been given (except as otherwise expressly set forth herein) if given by personal delivery on actual delivery during normal business hours, if given by registered prepaid airmail seven days after posting, if given by telex one Business Day after dispatch, and if given by cable two Business Days after dispatch. Any notice shall be addressed and sent to a party at its address set forth on the signature pages hereto, or at such other address as the recipient may have notified to the other.

Section 6.02. Delays, etc. No failure or delay in exercising any right, power or privilege hereunder shall operate as a waiver thereof nor shall any single or partial exercise of any right, power or privilege preclude any other or further exercise thereof, or the exercise of any other right, power or privilege.

Section 6.03. Reimbursement of Expenses. [The Company agrees to pay all costs and expenses (and any value added tax thereon) incurred by the Bank in connection with the preparation and execution of this Agreement, including without limitation the fees and expenses of legal advisers to the Bank.] Each party agrees to reimburse the other for actual expenses, including legal fees and expenses, reasonably incurred by the other in contemplation of or otherwise in connection with the enforcement of, or the preservation of any rights under, this Agreement. [The Company shall indemnify the Bank, upon demand by the Bank, against any present or future claim or liability for any stamp or other similar taxes and any penalties or interest with respect thereto, which may be assessed, levied or collected by any jurisdiction in connection with the performance by the Company of its obligations hereunder.]

Section 6.04. Execution, Amendments, Assignments and References. This Agreement may be executed in any number of counterparts and by the parties hereto in separate counterparts, each of which when so executed and delivered shall be deemed to be an original and all of which taken together shall constitute but one and the same instrument. No amendment, waiver, modification or supplement of any provision of this Agreement nor any consent to any departure therefrom shall in any event be effective unless in writing and signed by the parties. This Agreement shall be binding upon and inure to the benefit of the parties and their respective successors and assigns, *provided*, that [a party] [the Company] shall not be entitled to assign its rights hereunder (whether by security or otherwise) or any interest herein without the prior written consent of the [other party] [Bank], which consent shall not be unreasonably withheld. References herein to Articles, Sections and Schedules are to Articles, Sections and Schedules of this Agreement unless otherwise specified. Article and Section headings in this Agreement are included herein for convenience of reference only and shall not constitute a part of this Agreement for any other purpose. The Schedules shall be part of this Agreement and are hereby incorporated herein.

Section 6.05.   Determinations.   The Reference Bank shall make all determinations of amounts payable hereunder, unless otherwise expressly stated herein, each of which shall be conclusive and binding on the parties hereto in the absence of manifest error.

Section 6.06.   Governing law.   This Agreement shall be deemed to be a contract under, and this Agreement and the rights of the parties hereunder shall be governed by and construed and interpreted in accordance with, the laws of [the State of New York] [England].

Section 6.07.   Jurisdiction.   [Insert appropriate submission to jurisdiction depending on governing law and location of parties.]

Assignability and trading

With the increased volume of swaps which has occurred in the past year, increasing attention has been paid to the development of 'tradeable' swaps. The mutuality of obligations in swap agreements may prove an insurmountable obstacle to a true swaps 'security' which is freely tradeable. Swaps by their nature cannot be negotiable nor automatically assignable since the new party must assume the liability of the party whose rights are assigned and, presumably, an assigning party must be released from its obligations under the swap agreement. The remaining party to the agreement would generally wish to retain its rights against the assigning party, or alternately, make its own determination regarding the creditworthiness of the assignee. It is of course possible that one-sided swaps could evolve wherein a party would agree, on receipt of a flat payment in advance, to make future payments based on changes in interest rates. In addition, a central clearing exchange could be established which in effect would serve as an intermediary with the right to assign or trade its rights to receive payments. These forms would more closely resemble an interest option or future markets than true swaps.

Increased liquidity may, however, evolve in the swap market through other means. First, liquidity already exists to a certain extent due to the large number of participants in the swap industry and the ability to unwind a swap through writing a counter-swap. Thus, a party can 'trade' its position by writing a swap of a reverse nature. This does, however, leave that party with existing, and new, credit exposure.

Second, there may evolve a market in 'participations' in swaps. In this situation a party might write a single large swap agreement with one entity and sell participations therein to other entities. Such a sale would not, however, relieve the selling party from its liability to the first party, although the selling party could reduce its exposure to the first party by agreeing to pay over to the participants only those amounts which it actually receives from the first party.

Third, parties could agree in a swap agreement to a form of assignment and assumption document which either party could enter with any one of a preagreed list of major swap participants. This list could be subject to revision or confirmation on a periodic basis. In effect, then, either party could sign such a document with one of the preagreed entities with the effect that the assigning party would be released from its obligations and the new party would be fully bound under the swap agreement. Such a structure might present credit difficulties to certain entities. For instance, a bank or other regulated entity might not be able to agree in advance to an assignment to any one of a list of entities without its further consent, because of the requirements on it to monitor its credit exposure to any one party. In addition, there might well be anti-trust problems under the laws of various jurisdictions if such a system could be characterised as a closed group of trading entities.

Any system of increased liquidity will require greater standardisation of documentation. There are movements afoot among major swap participants to make documentation more standard. A number of US investment banks are attempting to coordinate such standardisation in order to improve liquidity. In addition, the British Bankers Association is reviewing the potential for standardisation in order to avoid misunderstanding of fundamental points when parties commit to transactions. On the other hand, the anti-trust laws of various jurisdictions may pose restrictions as to any efforts in this direction which might constitute a restraint on trade or exclusion of others from trading. In addition, financial institutions have traditionally evidenced a strong desire to use their own forms on a regular basis, even if the provisions are relatively similar in substance throughout the market.

Master agreements

One method of at least reducing paperwork has been the creation of master agreements or standard provisions, which are triggered or incorporated into short documents executed subsequently setting forth the business terms. For example, if two entities have written a number of swaps together and wish to expedite future transactions, they may agree on general provisions to govern their relationship, which will apply on a deal-by-deal basis subject to telex confirmation of the specifics of each deal (eg, payment dates, rates and notional principal amount).

GUARANTEES AND COLLATERAL

Due to the credit exposure discussed above, parties have sought means of reducing credit risk to one another. Part of the impetus for this derives also from the desire for increased liquidity in the market. The greater the credit support in a swap, the more likely it is that a swap could be assigned or a replacement party could be found. Credit support could derive from one or two sources: guarantees (or letters of credit) and collateral.

A guarantee may be effected by having the guarantor becoming a direct party jointly and severally obligated, having a separate guarantee or having a 'wraparound' agreement where the guarantor takes over the rights and obligations of the primary party on the termination of the primary party's rights and obligations. Guarantees run from full guarantees of all obligations, with the usual anti-release language, to short form guarantees of close-out payments.

This issue requires close attention to the insolvency laws of the jurisdiction of the primary obligor and how swap payments might be characterised in different types of proceedings. If the insolvent party fails to make a payment under the swap agreement, the solvent party would then call under the guarantee in respect of that payment, and assumedly the guarantor would pay it. On the next occasion on which the solvent party was obligated to make a payment under the swap agreement, that payment would go to the insolvent party. Thus, a pattern would develop where the guarantor was making payments to the solvent party and the insolvent party was receiving the payments from the solvent party. The guarantor would receive only rights of subrogation against the insolvent party (which may have some priority, however, in certain jurisdictions). If the parties inserted a provision in the swap agreement that on payment by the guarantor, all subsequent payments by the other party would be made to the guarantor, such a provision would be subject to the problems discussed above regarding the right in certain jurisdictions of a solvent party to terminate the agreement as against an insolvent party. Thus, it is safest for the guarantor to guarantee only the close-out amount. The beneficiary of the guarantee, however, would prefer that it be entitled to continue the agreement and that it not be forced to close out the agreement in order to realise on the guarantee.

The letter of credit avoids certain of the aforementioned difficulties. However, the party obligated on the letter of credit would not, after payment, have rights to subrogation. It would look solely to the party whose obligations were supported by the letter of credit for indemnification. In order to prevent the cost of such a letter of credit from being prohibitive if acquired from a third party, the letter of credit would have to be in a limited amount, probably keyed into the close-out payment required under the agreement.

Finally, one or both of the parties to an agreement could agree to make available collateral of a predetermined nature at the request of the other party based on exposure at any given time calculated by reference to the close-out provisions of the agreement. Such provisions are subject to several weaknesses. First, certain entities (such as banks and other regulated companies) have limitations on their power to grant security. Others may be restricted in granting security by negative pledge clauses of other agreements. An agreement to provide a letter of credit in lieu of collateral may well result in an expense (eg, the cost of obtaining the letter of credit) which reduces the desirability of the swap agreement.

Second, contract terms requiring provisions to give collateral are unlikely to be specifically enforceable. The agreement to provide collateral is not of itself collateral. A party's refusal to provide collateral under the terms of the agreement a failure would be a breach of the agreement entitling the other party to close the agreement out, but such close-out would be on an unsecured basis. If the agreement to provide collateral is based on certain objective or subjective evaluations of the current credit standing of a party, the provision thus becomes a subtle material adverse change clause by another name. If the provision is not based on a change in creditworthiness but is at the option of either party at any time, substantial questions would arise based on the cost to a party of an arbitrary (but permissible) call under the provisions and threats to liquidity on the part of an entity which had entered into a substantial number of swaps containing such provisions.

CONCLUSION

Swap documentation, while in many respects becoming increasingly standardised, is still rapidly evolving. It can be expected to evolve further with the creation of new forms of swap financing, the increased number of participants and new applications. This evolution may present further legal questions which have not yet been discussed. For instance, are swaps (or will swaps evolve into) securities, subject to the laws of the various jurisdictions regarding securities transactions? If the swaps market develops on a closed basis, would anti-trust questions relating to anti-competitive practices and monopolisation apply to the limited number of players at the core of the market? If swap documentation becomes too standardised, how is it keyed into the differing nature of the assets and liabilities which are hedged in respect of payment mechanisms, payment dates and the different practices of different capital markets?

CHAPTER 8

Accounting treatment

The purpose of this chapter is to consider the accounting principles and methods appropriate for recording and measuring various types of currency swaps. The basic purpose of any swap is to take advantage of the different financial capabilities of two entities to the mutual benefit of both parties involved, by reducing the inherent risks or costs of certain financial transactions. The problems of accounting for swaps primarily arise from the need to prepare periodic financial statements. Over the full life of a swap its total financial consequences on the entity arising from exchange rate movements, interest and other costs will be reflected in cash flow and the ultimate net cash flow will reveal the total profit or loss on the transaction. It is the allocation of this profit or loss between accounting periods and, where necessary, its estimation in advance of the ultimate outcome, that we need to consider here.

In accounting for any transaction the following four basic concepts will underlie the chosen treatment:

1 *Going concern* – In normal circumstances accounts should be prepared on the assumption that the entity will continue in activity for the foreseeable future. As applied to swaps this means that, unless there is evidence to the contrary, transactions not completed at the balance sheet date should be valued on the basis that there will not be a forced realisation.

2 *Accruals (or 'matching')* – Revenue and costs should be taken up in the accounts as they arise, and not only when they are finally reflected in cash flows. In addition, revenues should be matched with related costs. We should, therefore, aim for accounting methods which spread the net result of the swap over the period in which benefit is received. Where two individual transactions comprise a swap, one of which gives rise to an overall profit and the other an overall loss, their financial results should be matched, except that provision should be made for any net loss.

3 *Consistency* – Any accounting method should be applied consistently from one period to the next to enable the reader of the accounts to make meaningful comparisons.

4 *Prudence* – Revenues should not be recorded before their ultimate realisation is reasonably certain; similarly provision should be made for all expected costs and losses. The application of prudence necessarily involves a substantial amount of management judgement and, in the case of swaps, will often depend on the detailed circumstances surrounding each individual transaction.

In applying these above concepts the aim should always be to reflect in the accounts the economic reality of what management is doing and the impact of the swap on current and future cash flows.

BACK-TO-BACK AND PARALLEL LOANS

The accounting treatment of back-to-back and parallel loans should be similar to the treatment adopted for any other unhedged foreign currency, asset or liability. In the UK, at the balance sheet date the loans payable and receivable should be translated into local currency at the relevant spot rate and the translation gain or loss taken to the profit and loss account.

This may be illustrated through the use of the same example for both a back-to-back and a parallel loan.

1 Back-to-back loan (Exhibit 1)

(1) A US company lends a French company $10,000,000 on 1 January for five years at a rate of 11% per annum. The asset is recorded at its face value in the US company's accounts. At the same time the French company lends FFr75,000,000 to the US company for five years at 15% per annum. This is translated at the current spot rate of $1 = FFr7.5 and recorded as a liability in the books of the US company.

(2) At 30 June, the balance sheet date, the borrowings are retranslated at the spot rate ruling at that date, $1 = FFr7.25. This produces an exchange loss of $344,827 which is taken to the profit and loss account. In addition, the accrued interest receivable and payable is set up in the accounts. The accrued interest payable on the French Franc loan is translated at the spot rate $1 = FFr7.25.

(3) If a right of set-off is included in the loan agreement, the loan and the borrowings, together with the related interest, may be netted for the purposes of balance sheet presentation. However, if no legal right of set-off exists, the amounts must be shown gross.

2 Parallel loans (Exhibit 2)

(1) A US parent company lends $10,000,000 to a French company's US subsidiary for five years at 11% per annum. The loan is recorded in at its face value in the books of the US company. At the same time the French parent company lends FFr75,000,000 to a French subsidiary of the US parent company for five years at 15% per annum. The liability is recorded in the subsidiary's books and translated at the spot rate ruling on 1 January, $1 = FFr7.5.

(2) The French Franc borrowings are retranslated at the spot rate ruling on 20 June, $1 = FFr7.25. This gives an exchange loss of $344,827 which is taken to profit and loss.

(3) Accrued interest receivable and payable is set up as a sundry debtor and creditor. The accrued interest payable is translated at the spot rate of $1 = FFr7.25.

(4) Again, the principal amount and interest may be netted off on consolidation if a right of set-off is included in the parallel loan agreement.

The only difference between the treatment of the back-to-back loan and the parallel loan is that one takes place solely in the books of one company whilst the other is recorded in the books of two companies. The net effect in the consolidated accounts is the same in the two cases.

EXHIBIT 1 – BACK-TO-BACK LOANS

	FFr		US$				
	Creditors	Borrowings	Debtors	Creditors	Loans	Borrowings	Profit and loss
Books of US company							
DR/(CR)							
(1) 1 January Loan Borrowings	10,000,000	(75,000,000) @ 7.25			10,000,000	(10,000,000)	
(2) 30 June Revaluation of borrowings	10,344,827	(75,000,000) @ 7.25					
Exchange loss	344,827					(344,827)	344,827
Accrued interest: £10,000,000 × 11% ×6/12			550,000				(550,000)
FFr75,000,000 × 15% ×6/12 (5,625,000) @ 7.25				(775,862)			775,862
(3) Set off (if applicable)			(550,000)	550,000	(10,000,000)	10,000,000	
Balance sheet totals			—	(225,862)	—	(344,827)	570,689

In some situations, an entity may decide to hedge the future foreign currency cash flow resulting from its obligations to repay the foreign currency loans which it has received. If this is so, it is more appropriate to translate the loan at the rate fixed in the hedging contract. Any exchange gain or loss arising through the difference between the spot rate at the date the loan was granted and the rate fixed by the hedging contract should be taken to the profit and loss account evenly over the term of the loan.

INTEREST RATE OR COUPON SWAPS

In an interest rate swap, the two parties will typically have borrowed the same principal amounts in the same currency for the same period of time, one borrowing at a fixed rate and the other at a floating rate. Under the terms of the swap each party agrees to pay the interest costs on the other party's borrowings. This is effected by means of net payments between the parties.

Accounting for this type of swap is straightforward. Each party continues to carry its own loan in its balance sheet. In addition its profit or loss account is charged with the interest cost of its own loan plus or minus any amounts due from or to the other swap party calculated on an accruals basis. Thus the net amount charged to the profit or loss account in any one period is equivalent to the interest cost on the other party's borrowings. Any fees or commissions are charged to the profit and loss account on a normal accruals basis.

Exhibit 3 gives an example.

(1) A company borrows $50 million on 1 January at a fixed rate of 11% per annum, enters into a swap with company B whereby company A agrees to pay the interest on company B's borrowings, also $50 million at a floating rate of LIBOR less $\frac{1}{2}$%. In return, company B agrees to pay interest on company A's borrowings at 11%. On initiation, the swap agreement has no accounting implications.

(2) Company A has a year end on 31 March. At this date it therefore accrues for three months interest on its borrowings.

(3) For the first six months of the agreement, LIBOR is 12%. At 31 March company A sets up an accrual of $62,500 being the net amount payable under the swap agreement (three months interest differential between the fixed rate of 11% and the variable rate of LIBOR $-\frac{1}{2}$%). Company A therefore suffers interest at an effective rate of LIBOR $-\frac{1}{2}$%.

(4) (a) On 30 June company A accrues a further three months interest on its borrowings.
    (b) The half yearly interest payment on the borrowing is paid.
    (c) Company A also pays the net amount due under the interest rate swap to company B. The portion already accrued is charged to creditors whilst the remainder is charged to profit and loss account.

(5) The next six months LIBOR is 11%. On 31 December company A pays the next half yearly interest charge in the borrowings and receives $125,000 from company B under the terms of the interest rate swap.

(6) For the next six months LIBOR is $10\frac{1}{2}$%. At the year end an accrual for the interest payable on the borrowing is again made. Also a debtor is set up for the amount receivable under the interest rate swap.

EXHIBIT 2 – PARALLEL LOANS

Books of US parent company

US$

	Debtors	Creditors	Loans	Borrowings	Cash	Profit and loss
(1) 1 January Loan			10,000,000		(10,000,000)	
(3) 30 June Accrued interest = £10,000,000 × 11% × 6/12	550,000					(550,000)
Balance sheet totals	550,000	—	10,000,000	—	(10,000,000)	(550,000)

Books of French subsidiary of US parent company

		Debtors	Creditors	Loans	Borrowings	Cash	Profit and loss
(1) 1 January Borrowing	10,000,000	(75,000,000) @ 7.5				(10,000,000)	10,000,000
(2) 30 June Revaluation of borrowings	10,344,827	(75,000,000) @ 7.25				(344,827)	
Exchange loss	344,827						344,827
carried forward		—	—		(10,344,827)	10,000,000	344,827

EXHIBIT 2 – PARALLEL LOANS (CONTINUED)

	FFr		Debtors	Creditors	Loans	Borrowings	Cash	US$ Profit and loss
	Creditors	Borrowings						
brought forward								
(3) 30 June								
Accrued interest =								
FFr75,000,000 × 15%	(5,625,000)			(775,862)				775,862
× 6/12	@ 7.25							
Balance sheet								
totals			—	(775,862)	—	(10,344,827)	10,000,000	1,120,689
Consolidated accounts								
			550,000	(775,862)	10,000,000	(10,344,827)	(10,000,000)	(550,000)
(4) Set off			(550,000)	550,000	(10,000,000)	10,000,000	10,000,000	1,120,689
Balance sheet								
totals			—	(225,862)	—	(344,827)	—	570,689

EXHIBIT 3 – INTEREST RATE OR COUPON SWAPS

DR/(CR)	Borrowings $	Debtors $	Creditors $	Cash $	Profit or loss $
Company A					
(1) January					
$50,000,000 borrowed	(50,000,000)			50,000,000	
Interest rate swap entered into – no accounting effect					
(2) 31 March					
Interest (payable) on loan					
11% × $50,000,000 × 3/12			(1,375,000)		1,375,000
(3) Accrued swap payment					
Due to bank B =					
$50,000,000 × 11.5% × 3/12 = $1,437,500					
Due from bank B =					
$50,000,000 × 11% × 3/12 = $1,375,000					
$62,500			(62,500)		62,500
Balance sheet totals – year 1	(50,000,000)	—	(1,437,500)	50,000,000	1,437,500
Brought forward	(50,000,000)		(1,437,500)	50,000,000	1,437,500
(4) 30 June					
(a) Interest on bank loan for three months = $50,000,000 × 11% × 3/12			(1,375,000)		1,375,000
(b) Payment of interest on bank loan for six months			2,750,000	(2,750,000)	
carried forward	(50,000,000)	—	(62,500)	47,250,000	2,813,500

EXHIBIT 3 – INTEREST RATE OR COUPON SWAPS (CONTINUED)

DR/(CR)	*Borrowings* $	*Debtors* $	*Creditors* $	*Cash* $	*Profit or loss* $
brought forward	(50,000,000)	—	(62,500)	47,250,000	2,813,500
(c) Payment under swap agreement					
Due to B: $50,000,000 × 11.5% × 6/12 = $2,875,000					
Due from B: $50,000,000 × 11% × 6/12 = $2,750,000					
$125,000					
(5) 31 December					
(a) Interest on bank loan = $50,000,000 × 11% × 6/12			62,500	(125,000)	62,500
(b) Receipt under swap agreement					
Due to B: $50,000,000 × 10½% × 6/12 = $2,625,000				(2,750,000)	2,750,000
Due from B: $50,000,000 × 11% × 6/12 = $2,750,000					
$125,000		125,000		125,000	(125,000)
(6) 31 March					
(a) Interest payable on bank loan = $50,000,000 × 11% × 3/12			(1,375,000)		1,375,000
(b) Accrued swap receipt					
Due to B: $50,000,000 × 10½% × 3/12 = $1,250,000					
Due from B: $50,000,000 × 11% × 3/12 = $1,375,000		125,000			(125,000)
$125,000					
Balance sheet totals – year 2	(50,000,000)	125,000	(1,375,000)	44,500,000	6,750,000

CROSS-CURRENCY FIXED-TO-FIXED SWAP

In a cross-currency fixed-to-fixed swap, the two parties agree to service each other's borrowings by making both interest and capital payments on each other's behalf. Thus party A bears the cost of interest and exchange movements, if any, on party B's loan and these costs are reflected in party A's profit and loss account. Similarly, party B services party A's loan in the same way. In addition there would be a fee payable between the parties to compensate for the interest rate differential between the currencies.

In spite of the swap agreement, each party still retains a legal obligation to ensure that its own source of finance is repaid and hence each party will translate its own loan at the spot rate prevailing at the balance sheet date. The difference between each party's capital obligation to repay the other party's loan, and its own loan translated at spot rate, will be held in a suspense account until the end of the swap transaction.

The treatment may be illustrated by means of the example set out in Exhibit 4.

CROSS-CURRENCY FIXED-TO-FIXED SWAPS (exhibit 4)

DR/(CR)	Borrowings £	Debtor £	Creditor £	Profit or loss £
UK company				
(1) 1 January				
Borrow $10,000,000				
when exchange rate				
is £1 = $1.45	(6,896,552)			
(2) 31 December				
Accrue interest on				
US company's loan			(758,621)	758,621
(3) Revalue dollar				
loan at spot				
$10,000,000 @				
$1.4 = £1	7,142,857			
Previous valuation	6,896,552			
	$246,305			
	(246,305)	246,305		
Balance sheet totals	7,142,857	246,305	(758,621)	758,621

(1) A UK company borrows $10,000,000 at an interest rate of 11% per annum on 1 January when the exchange rate is £1 = $1.45. At the same time a US company borrows £6,896,522 also at 11% per annum. The two parties enter into a fixed-to-fixed cross currency debt swap. The swap agreement does not generate any accounting entries at this time.

(2) At 31 December, the balance sheet date, each party charges its profit and loss account with the cost of the interest on the other party's loan. Thus the UK company bears the interest on the US company's loan.

(3) The loan principal is revalued at the spot rate ruling at the balance sheet date (£1 = $1.4). However, under the terms of the swap agreement, the exchange difference will be covered by the US company. It is therefore transferred to a debtor account rather than to profit and loss.

In accounting for a cross-currency swap it is particularly important to consider the credit risk inherent in the swap transaction. Usually there will be an effective right of set off in the agreement so that if one party defaults on its payments, then the other party may cease making its payments and will then resume making payments to its original source of finance. If such a default appears probable, and the other party is unable to pay, it may be necessary for the non defaulting party to provide for the exchange exposure that would result from it being forced to resume payments in the currency of its borrowings.

Occasionally, there will be no such right of set off in the swap agreements so that one party could possibly find itself paying both obligations. In this case the total obligations under the other party's loan would be charged to profit.

CROSS-CURRENCY FIXED.TO FLOATING SWAPS

This type of transaction is exactly the same as the cross-currency fixed-to-fixed swap except that one party has a fixed rate loan and the other a floating rate loan. The accounting is therefore similar to that used for the fixed-to-fixed cross currency debt swap. Each party charges its own profit and loss account with the other party's interest cost. In addition, each party compensates the other for the effect of exchange rate movements on the principal of the loan.

OTHER SWAPS

Two further types of swap are the same-currency and cross-currency floating-to-floating rate swaps. The accounting methods appropriate to these transactions follow closely those outlined above.

CHAPTER 9

Future developments

In the introduction we listed a number of applications of the swap product. The case studies were chosen not only to show the different forms of swaps but also to illustrate the applications. It should now be apparent that the permutations and combinations for applying the swap product expand with each new innovation in the capital markets and that new opportunities arise every time an anomaly is discovered.

It is the exploitation of an anomaly and its problem-solving ability which is the driving force behind swap financing. For example, the overall spread differential between the European capital market and the bank credit market drives the typical fixed-rate/LIBOR interest rate swap. Other anomalies, such as the European banks' preference for LIBOR-priced assets as opposed to prime-priced assets, the Swiss capital markets appetite for US industrial names and US accounting regulations allowing foreign exchange losses to be deducted from reserves as opposed to being a charge against the profit and loss statement, will ensure the continued growth of swap financing and development of further applications. Events such as World Bank's decision to use its floating-rate dollar borrowing ability for swapping purposes in order to generate simulated fixed-rate liabilities in the low interest currencies will also facilitate future development.

A set of circumstances could develop under which the swap product may become superfluous. Currently, the options and future markets only go out two to three years and foreign exchange markets in the major currencies three to five years. The securities markets tend to go out from three to twenty years although in recent years, except for sterling and dollars where availability is limited, capital markets have tended to shorten to seven to ten years. The swap has filled this maturity gap. However, with securities markets getting shorter in maturity and forward foreign exchange, options and future markets getting longer, what can today be achieved through a swap may be achieved through an option futures or forward foreign exchange contract in the future.

However, the two matrices set out below lend an insight into the variety of possible future developments. The first matrix lists across and down the page various methods of pricing floating rate debt instruments. Through

MATRIX I	*LIBOR*	*Prime*	*B.A.*	*Fed. Funds*	*T. Bills*	*CP*
Libor						
Prime						
B.A.						
Fed. Funds						
T. Bills						
CP						

use of the interest rate swap, it should be possible to arbitrage anomalies or exploit individual strengths and weaknesses between, eg, the commercial paper market and the bank credit market for prime priced assets. A review of the possible combinations revealed by the first matrix and comparison with the types of swaps so far undertaken will indicate that there is still potential for further innovation in, development of and application for swap financings.

The second matrix considers various types of fixed-rate instruments in the same way. Again, the matrix will reveal many permutations and combinations. If one were to combine both matrices, future possibilities are expanded even further.

MATRIX II	Fixed Rate	With Warrants	Zero Coupon	Convertible	Preference Stock
Fixed rate					
With warrants					
Zero coupon					
Convertible					
Preference stock					

If one were then to insert the currency factor, eg, dollars, pounds sterling, Dutch guilders, Deutschemarks and Swiss francs, the possibilities become practically infinite.

It is easy to hypothesise on the above basis, but one has to be practical and realistic. To illustrate the practicality of certain combinations, the following is an example of a 'cocktail' swap which contains three major types of swaps. It requires a bank to act as an intermediary.

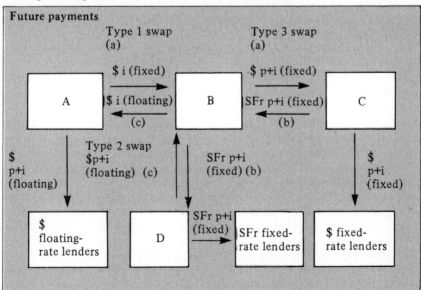

The benefits of the cocktail swap are as follows. The less creditworthy borrower A uses its ability to borrow floating-rate dollars to simulate a fixed-rate dollar liability via a coupon swap (Type 1). The strong borrower C uses its strength in the dollar capital market, which is greater than in the Swiss franc market, to borrow fixed-rate dollars to simulate a fixed Swiss franc liability via a cross-currency fixed-to-fixed debt swap (Type 3). The strong borrower D uses its ability to borrow fixed-rate Swiss francs in the Swiss franc capital market to simulate a floating-rate (below market) dollar liability via a cross-currency fixed-to-floating debt swap (Type 2).

B's role in the transaction is that of intermediary and arranger. It writes all contracts as principal, each contract standing alone. The identities of A, C and D remain unknown to one another.

Some of the more recent developments have been touched on already in this book. However, it is worth considering briefly some of these newer developments in order to stimulate thought as to what actually may be possible in the future.

NEW APPLICATIONS

Floating/floating swaps

1985 should see rapid development of the floating/floating swap. This may well become an individual product area in its own right with specialists developing solely in this area. The introduction of the reset, six-month LIBOR, calculated weekly but paid semi-annually, has already taken place. There is now a ready market for prime and LIBOR swaps. Ninety-day Treasury notes reset weekly are also proving fashionable as a pricing mechanism.

Currency/commodity swaps

According to market sources, the German power companies have been raising finance for the Austrian power companies and the Austrian power companies are re-paying the German power companies by selling them electricity in the future.

Energy price swap agreements

Both developers of energy sources (oil, gas, coal, uranium) and major users of energy (public and private utility companies, large manufacturing complexes) face the dilemma of making substantial long-term capital investments, the success of which is to a significant degree a function of future energy prices. Energy prices in the past decade have been notoriously volatile. This volatility is generally expected to continue. Developers and users now seek to reduce the impact of such volatility on their long-term capital investment decision-making processes primarily by negotiating long-term supply agreements. The importance of take-or-pay contracts to the financing of almost any major new energy pipeline project is but one example of this phenomenon.

Swap techniques appear to offer another, potentially more flexible, means of mitigating the volatility of energy prices. For example, by using swap techniques a user of energy might bear the risk of energy prices dropping below a stated level in exchange for a developer of energy sources bearing the risk of energy prices rising above the agreed level. Alternatively the shifted risk might relate to changes in the spread between the cost of energy derived from two different sources (eg, coal, oil or gas versus uranium).

The two parties to the agreement might, for example, agree to pay each other on a periodic basis gross amounts, equivalent to the price of a notional amount of energy (eg, X barrels of oil) determined on the basis in the first party's (eg, the user's) case that the price per unit of energy was Y and in the second party's (eg, the developer's) case that the price per unit was a specified floating rate (eg, the price on the Rotterdam market).

Arbitraging FX markets

One anomaly which is only beginning to be exploited arises from the common practice of banks quoting the same forward foreign exchange rates to all clients. The potential scope for arbitraging the bank foreign exchange market against the various capital markets has barely been tapped. For example, a number of the Swiss franc dual currency issues have been hedged profitably against the forward foreign exchange market.

FUTURE OF THE PRODUCT

A major drawback to swaps is that they are non-callable during their life, unlike a bond issue which may have a prepayment right. Today, this is no longer a major problem because of the liquidity in the swap market. If a company wants to unwind a swap, it simply writes a reverse swap.

Liquidity has come about for a number of reasons. First, volume: in 1983 it was conservatively estimated that some $20 billion in interest rate swaps were written and $6 billion in currency swaps. Actual figures may have been as high as $30 billion and $10 billion, respectively. Estimates in respect of 1984 have ranged as high as 100 billion for interest swaps.

Second, a number of banks, such as Citibank, Chase Manhattan Bank, Morgan and First Interstate, have started warehousing activities, in effect becoming quasi-market makers in swaps. For example, a bank can buy a swap where it will pay fixed and receive floating. It will then either buy a matching US Treasury bond or enter into a futures contract. When it effectively on-sells its swap position to, say, a weaker credit such as a US utility, under which the utility would pay fixed and receive floating, at the same time it would sell the US Treasury bonds or close out its futures contract. Profits or losses on the hedge would be treated as costs of running the warehousing operation, and amortised over the life of the underlying swap or swaps.

As a result of these activities, a number of banks are now prepared to quote a two-way price for swaps. For example, the price for a five-year fixed/six-month LIBOR dollar swap would be quoted as five-year Treasuries plus 65/75 basis points. This means a bank would buy a swap subject to the creditworthiness of the counterparty, under which it would pay fixed and receive floating (six months LIBOR), with the fixed rate being the current yield to maturity on the selected or reference five-year US Treasury bond plus 65 basis points.

Some of the large investment banks, such as Salomon Brothers, have also started similar market-making activities. With approximately one in three Eurobond issues being swap related, the major security issuing houses such as Credit Suisse First Boston, Morgan Stanley, Warburgs and others will be forced into this market-making role in order to protect and promote their lead management activities.

The most recent entrants into the market have been the money brokers who are linking their deposit-broking activities with swap transactions. The market has gained such depth and volume as to permit brokerage operations to thrive.

As discussed above in Chapter 7, efforts are being made to standardise swap documentation and to create tradeable swaps or swaps with an increased likelihood of assignability. Such assignability would greatly increase the attractiveness of swaps.

The above innovations and developments result from the ingenuity of corporate finance experts. Their efforts to solve their clients' problems should further fuel expansion of the swap product. Every time interest rates, exchange rates and government regulations change, new anomalies occur which most probably can be exploited through using swap financing techniques.

Index